A Bite-Sized Public Affairs Book

The BBC – A Winter of Discontent?

Edited by

John Mair

Cover by

Dean Stockton

Published by Bite-Sized Books Ltd 2020

Bite-Sized Books Ltd Cleeve Road, Goring RG8 9BJ UK information@bite-sizedbooks.com

Registered in the UK. Company Registration

No: 9395379

ISBN: 9798694863117

The moral right of John Mair to be identified as the author of this work has been asserted by him in accordance with the Copyright, Designs and Patents

Act 1988

Contents

***

Who Pays the Piper and Who Plays the Tune?

***

How Big a BBC?

***

News: Impartiality, Enemies, Balance, 'Troubles' BAME and Wise Men

Acknowledgments

As always, this book is only as good as the contributions. I am hugely grateful to the twenty authors who delivered superb copy on time. Nobody is paid, especially not me. They write because they care about the subject and want to make a sensible public intervention into a crucial national debate. They deserve huge kudos.

So too (one of) my long suffering publishers Paul Davies of Bite-Sized books and the brilliant genius of Dean Stockton for another superb cover. Look at it closely - work out the semiotics. . . .

Enjoy the book. Let's hope it makes a splash and has some good effect.

John Mair

Jericho Oxford. October 1st 2020

The Editor

This is John Mair's thirty seventh 'hackademic' book in the last decade or more. Seven this year alone. This the third in the BBC In Peril series, three on the Pandemic and the media and one on the coming oil boom in *Oil Dorado* – Guyana. More to come with a big book on Donald Trump, Boris Johnson and populism due in 2021.

He is a one person book factory.

In previous lives, John was a television producer/director for the BBC,ITV and Channel Four, a university lecturer and a schoolteacher.

He is always open to new ideas for books and new authors.

johnmair100@hotmail. com twitter@johnmair10F

Foreword

Rottweiler 1 interviews Rottweiler 2

John Humphrys

John Humphrys is the BBC Rottweiler in retirement. He retired from 'Today' after 22 years in October 2019, 54 years in the Corporation. Here the great interviewer interviews…himself.. about the BBC.

JH: So… we meet again. A whole year without hearing your truculent tones on *Today*. They seem to have managed perfectly well without you.

JH: Of course. There was never any doubt about that. I was one presenter among many.

JH: Very noble but I bet you're missing them.

JH: Quite the opposite. I won't pretend I haven't screamed at the radio from time to time, but I've made the amazing discovery that there may be more to life than arguing with politicians.

JH: Fifty years with the BBC, and you're honestly telling me you were able to pack it in without so much as a backward glance? I don't believe it!

JH: That's because you never believe anything. But I'm still broadcasting and . . .

JH: . . . oh sure . . . *Classic FM*! Not exactly T*oday* is it?

JH: No, thank God! If you had a straight choice between listening to Mozart at 8.10am and listening to the Minister For Never Answering a Straight Question . . .

JH: . . . as you well know that's a silly comparison. But you'll seize on any excuse to attack the BBC even though it gave you a bloody good living.

JH: That's nonsense. I was critical of some big bosses but I still believe the BBC is the most important cultural and democratic institution this country has ever produced and . . .

JH: . . . oh really? If that's true how do you explain the front page headline in the Daily Mail the day after you left New Broadcasting House? 'BBC ICON SAVAGES BIAS . . . AT THE BEEB'!

JH: I stand by every word. The BBC has had problems with bias in many areas even though it has an absolute obligation to remain impartial.

JH: So why didn't you make a fuss at the time?

JH: I did. I just didn't go public. You cannot continue to work for an organisation if you're publicly attacking it.

JH: Ah . . . so if it's a choice between speaking out publicly for what matters and clinging on to your fat pay cheque, you'll take the money and stay shtum.

JH: I concede that's how it might look but if every senior figure at the BBC who had misgivings about its conduct were to walk out, there'd be many empty chairs on the News Board.

JH: All the better for that . . .

JH: Possibly. But my worry is that, in the year since I left, BBC News has come under unprecedented pressure from activists determined to impose their own political agenda.

JH: I could almost hear the sneer when you used the word 'activists'! I assume you're referring to people from the black and ethnic minority community who've been seriously discriminated against for generations. Not to mention the LGBTQ community.

JH: No 'sneer' but, yes, I'm uneasy with the language. Many black and gay people are insulted by the notion that they are members of a 'community'. It suggests that they have no individual opinions or experiences of their own and see themselves as victims. They're not and they don't.

JH: So you'd be happy for the BBC to return to the Sixties? I bet the only black people you ever saw then were cleaners and all the bosses were straight white men.

JH: God forbid! They were indeed bad days. But the BBC was hardly unique in racially discriminating. It was reflecting the nation. I was brought up in what would certainly be regarded now as a racist household in a racist area. My parents had not a single neighbour, let alone friend, who was black. And as for a black woman or even a white woman reading the news on the wireless, let alone the telly . . . dream on!

JH: In which case why have you been attacking the BBC for its coverage of the *Black Lives Matter* movement, to name just one example?

JH: What I have attacked is the way the BBC has failed too often in its duty to be totally objective on many controversial issues such as immigration and the EU, or even the *Last Night of the Proms* fiasco. It is not the BBC's job to transform society in ways that will meet the approval of certain pressure groups.

JH: Not even if those pressure groups are on the side of the angels?

JH: Not even then. No. And let's not forget that *BLM* in this country is a political movement with objectives many people regard as profoundly disturbing — such as 'defunding' the police and closing the prisons.

JH: The fact is you'd be happy if we still tolerated racism or prejudice against gay people and still had laws, for instance, making it illegal for a man to sleep with another man?

JH: Don't be ridiculous. That law was an obscenity. And it changed because the men and women we sent to Parliament voted for the change. And, yes, they came under pressure, but it was not pressure from the BBC. It was pressure from the victims of that hideously outdated and iniquitous law and their supporters who marched in the streets and demanded reform and won the support of the majority of British citizens. It's called the democratic process. And the BBC reported that great campaign because that was its duty. And is still its duty.

JH: Very high-minded no doubt, but not even the BBC can be impartial where racism is concerned.

JH: Tell me about it. I lived for years in South Africa. I saw the evil of apartheid at first hand and I reported what I saw. That's what journalists do. We report the facts.

JH: And one fact is that there is still racism in this country and the BBC has an obligation to report it.

JH: True, but there are now laws which make it illegal and when those laws are broken the BBC does indeed report it. The same applies to sexuality. It's illegal to discriminate against gays or lesbians or transgender people and the BBC's reporting must reflect that.

JH: In which case why did you attack the BBC for appointing an LGBT correspondent?

JH: I didn't. I attacked it for giving him a platform on which he said he regarded himself as a 'mouthpiece' for LGBT people. He's not. He's a journalist.

JH: One single example of some loose language is hardly evidence of the BBC allowing its reporters and correspondents to set their own agenda.

JH: You want another? Since I wrote the book (*A Day like Today*), the BBC has also appointed a 'gender and identity' correspondent. She became involved in a massive row when she attacked the decision of a television news reporter to use the 'N-word' in a report about a serious racist attack on a young black man.

JH: Quite right, too. Everyone knows that word is simply unacceptable in this day and age.

JH: Fair enough, but in this case the young man's mother wanted the word to be used because it proved the attack really was racially-motivated. The police changed the charge from 'hit and run' to 'racially motivated attack'. And the reporter warned the audience she was going to use an offensive word. So did the presenters.

JH: But I bet the audience was massively offended.

JH: That's what was so interesting. When the report was shown on *Points West* there were a handful of complaints. But by the time it was repeated the following morning on the BBC's national news the Twitter mob and the lobby groups were on the case. They screamed blue murder and the BBC started to panic.

A week later Tony Hall, who was director general then, called a meeting of the top bosses on a Sunday and the position he'd originally taken was reversed. The BBC apologised.

JH: And so he should have. You can't go around offending thousands of people without saying sorry — even if you are the almighty BBC.

JH: Rubbish! Thousands of people are offended every day by stuff the BBC reports. There'd be something wrong if they were not.

JH: But only if what you're reporting is important . . .

JH: . . . which is precisely what Lord Hall said this was. I quote: 'This is important journalism which the BBC should be reporting on and we will continue to do so.' But then he flatly contradicted that by adding: 'I recognise that we have ended up creating distress among many people.'

So in other words the BBC will continue to do 'important journalism' just so long as it doesn't 'create distress'. That is neither rational nor acceptable. How do they deal with, say, low-life scum who deface a Holocaust memorial? Reporting it will cause distress among vast numbers of people (not just Jews) so should it be ignored?

JH: Of course not. But the BBC must take into account people's feelings.

JH: Really? Which people specifically? And who makes the ultimate decision?

JH: Well . . . BBC editors following the guidelines.

JH: Ah . . . we can agree on something. My real concern is that those guidelines are at risk of being hijacked by, among others, an organisation called *Embrace*, which the BBC recognises as the voice of black and ethnic minority staff and which is represented at high-level management meetings.

Embrace sent senior BBC bosses an internal document which included this line: 'We believe this to be a matter for debate within black communities, and not one for the BBC.' That is simply outrageous.

JH: Because?

JH: Because the BBC is responsible for all its editorial decisions. It cannot be excluded from the 'debate' by any special interest group. And God forbid it should allow words to be banned.

JH: Oh, come on. The fact is that the BBC took note of what its critics were saying and changed its mind. Maybe it should have done it more often in the past.

JH: But in my 50 years with the organisation there was never the sense that its senior management was being effectively held to ransom by people on its own staff in self-appointed 'advisory' groups who tell the bosses how things should be done.

They themselves have largely no editorial responsibility and they all have much the same agenda. They are, in the modern sense of the word, about as 'woke' as it gets. Since I left *Today* I have spoken to editors and very senior bosses who admit they feel intimidated. It has a chilling effect.

JH: You exaggerate again. There have always been pressure groups telling the BBC how it should report stories. What's different now?

JH: Social media for one thing. *Twitter* is a malign force. The BBC has fallen for the fiction that a few hundred attention-seeking, virtue-signalling agitators represent the conscience of the nation. They've allowed the woke whingers to frame the argument. That is profoundly worrying.

JH: Time for the BBC to call it a day then?

JH: Quite the opposite. The new Director General Tim Davie might well be its' saviour. In his first three days in the job he has reversed the ludicrous decision to wreck the *Last Night of the Proms* and has made a speech that had an old cynic like me cheering from the rafters.

He warned the ever-growing army of bureaucrats and bosses with silly titles to start looking for new jobs. He warned all those senior journalists who can't stay away from social media to keep their political views to themselves or clear off.

He warned recruiters to hire fewer metropolitan right-on Oxbridge types and find a few working-class youngsters who don't read only the *Guardian*. He wants to hear a few comics on Radio 4 who might (God forbid) have voted Conservative now and then.

He wants a 'radical shift . . . to focus on those we serve: the public'. He wants 'diversity of thought'. And — in some ways just as important — he has done something no previous DG has ever done.

He has recognised that the BBC is too big and must stop growing. Oh . . . and one other thing. He has put paid to the nonsense that the BBC might eventually become a subscription service like *Netflix.*

JH: Why nonsense?

JH: Because it would make it 'just another media company serving a specific group'.

JH: And the reaction to all this?

JH: Depends who you talk to but I'm already getting calls from some very senior figures who had drafted resignation letters and have now ripped them up.

JH: A bit naïve surely? He'll come under the same pressures that his predecessors have experienced.

JH: You bet! But if he chooses to fight he won't be alone. There are millions of decent people out there who share my fears. GK Chesterton identified them in his great poem called *The Secret People:*

Smile at us, pay us, pass us; but do not quite forget,

For we are the people of England, that never have spoken yet.

Adapted from *A Day Like Today* by John Humphrys, published in paperback by William Collins on October 1 2020.

About the Contributor

John Humphrys spent 54 years at the BBC as a reporter and presenter, latterly on Radio Four's *Today* programme for 22 years. He still presents *Mastermind.*

The Debates

Introduction

John Mair

Is the BBC in peril-you bet! Is it in for a winter of discontent with the government-you bet! Is it in for a rocky ride-fasten your seat belts!

Coming up to its centenary in 2022, more than ever before it faces an existential threat in the form of Boris Johnson and his brain/Svengali Dominic Cummings.

Week after week, they deliver massive warning shocks to the Corporation. Firstly, the threat to 'whack' them, then the 'consultation' on decriminalising non-payment of the licence fee – answer known before question put – and the latest bombshell – the 'done deal' of (Lord) Charles Moore, a convicted licence-fee refusenik, 'chosen' as the new Chair from 2021 with cover provided by the equally right-wing Paul Dacre as chair of the regulator *Ofcom.*

Incoming Director-General Tim Davie must wonder which mine field he has strayed into.

This is the third in the **IS THE BBC IN PERIL?** Bite Sized Books series this year. It is the most prescient and the most pressing. The books have set the agenda for the debate in 2020.They are read in high places.

This volume is full of discussion and disagreements. It is called democracy. Nowhere more so than in this opening section.

Fans, however critical, of the Corporation line up to defend it. Andrew Graham, who has spent a career studying broadcasting economics, demolishes the arguments against the hypothecated tax. Jean Seaton, the official BBC historian pronounces herself astonished at the sheer gall of the selection of a new Chairman by Downing Street leak, Ivor Gaber delves into the archives of a little known libertarian blog to ascertain what Dominic Cummings actually thinks about the BBC, Leighton Andrews, now a professor but formerly paid to defend the Corporation, frames the debate as part of the nascent 'Culture Wars' and as big a threat to the BBC as he can recall, Lindsay Mackie has set up and works for a group dedicated to *saveourbbc.* Ray Snoddy clearly lays out the challenges DG Davie faces.

The biggest enemies though are former friends. Rod Liddle was a senior BBC editor in radio-of the flagship *Today* programme some twenty years ago. Today he is firmly outside that tent plying his columnist trade on the right of the journalism spectrum at the *Spectator, Sunday Times* and *the Sun*. He firmly labels the BBC- as 'woke' (the modern Tory insult of choice), out of touch with 'the people' on Brexit and so much more. Like Robin Aitken later in this book Liddle is hoping for DG Davie to tilt the editorial balance dial towards the people, the right and, by the by, their view.

Hard debate and discussion is what is needed in these strange times. The BBC is still a national treasure like the NHS. It now needs much metaphorical clapping in living rooms each and every Thursday if it is to survive these attacks with its head and heart still intact. Winter has come early.

Chapter 1

Why We Need to Keep the BBC

Andrew Graham, the former Master of Balliol, uncovers the flaws in the multiple, ideologically driven attacks on the BBC and reminds us why we should not take it for granted but see it as a core part of our democracy, especially so in the new post-Enlightenment Age.

]

Introduction

The BBC is under attack. Even its friends are currently cross and disheartened. They see the BBC losing younger viewers, having a poor record on diversity, until recently underpaying its female employees, no longer having the edge in hard reporting, and, irrespective of the weight of evidence, being willing to regard two opposing voices as representing impartiality.

Then there are the ideological opponents opposed to the very idea of the BBC. As Barwise and York show,[1] over a long period, ideas promoted by American libertarian/free-market think tanks have been drip fed into a linked set of UK pressure groups, closely connected to Dominic Cummings. Naturally, the ideologues keep their fundamentalism mostly hidden, choosing instead to find arguments that might sway the friendly critics.

The flawed arguments

The first onslaught from the ideologues came in the Peacock Report (1986).[2] It stated, correctly, that the digital television removed the natural monopoly of the BBC, but went on to claim that, because television programmes *could* be sold, they *should* be sold.

Technical possibilities are, however, not necessarily, socially desirable.

---

[1] Barwise, Patrick and Peter York, The War against the BBC. Penguin Books (forthcoming)
[2] Peacock Committee (1986) Report of the Committee on the Financing of the BBC Cmnd.982444. London, HMSO

Today, cars easily exceed 100 mph, hardly desirable on public roads. Further, broadcasting is more like enjoying a National Park than car purchase. If I buy a car, you can't buy the same car, but if I walk in a park or watch a broadcast you can as well – at no extra cost. Just because tracking technology makes it possible to charge for every step in a National Park, does not make it anything other than idiotic to do so. As philosophers say, you cannot get an "ought" from and "is".

The second free-market critique comes in the claim that the BBC is too big for its boots and is "crowding out" the private market. Yet, the fact is that the BBC has shrunk.[3] In addition, the BBC has an obligation to "inform and educate" and this is because we watch or listen to broadcasts as citizens not just as consumers. And, without understanding our rights, we cannot even begin to function as "well-informed" consumers. In short, once the argument is clear, the argument of the critics is reversed. Far from the BBC cramping the market, it is a pre-requisite for the market.

Thirdly, it is argued that the arrival of the Internet and, still more so, the smartphone and social media make the BBC a total anachronism. With people able to obtain all the information, education and entertainment they want, wherever they are, why spend public money providing the BBC? The weakness is that this argument pre-supposes that people are always smart enough to distinguish truth from falsehood. This is manifestly not the case. Recent research[4] across the globe shows that 86% people think they were duped at least once in the preceding year. This has to be an underestimate since, by definition, we are unaware of the duping we do not spot! And, as Howard has shown,[5] as AI advances, this problem is set to grow substantially in scale and complexity.

Developments in social media further undermine the libertarian case. It is now widely recognised that, almost everywhere, internet use, social media use, misinformation, and fake news are on the rise. Social and political divisions are also on the rise, amplified by echo chambers. The implication of recent research[6] is that these developments are not chance, but *causally* related. It has always been the case that people like to interact with those of

---

[3] Even the argument that the BBC has become too big is false. In real terms, the BBC has shrunk by about one third in the last decade and, if it is forced to fund free licences for all over 75s and if the licence fee is decriminalised, it will shrink substantially further. Voice of the Listener and Viewer (2019)

[4] CIGI-Ipsos (2019)

[5] Howard, Philip (2020) Lie Machines: How to Save Democracy from Troll Armies, Deceitful Robots, Junk News Operations, and Political Operatives. Yale University Press

[6] See especially Pentland (2014) and the discussion in Syed (2019)

similar persuasions. What the Internet, and still more, social media have done is to make it trivially easy to find such people. Herein lies the factor creating echo chambers which then intensify social and political divisions (and vice versa). All this increases misinformation and fake news. If news, fake or otherwise, conforms to the expectations of those within any particular echo chamber, it is believed and passed on; whereas news which challenges the presumptions of the echo chamber is denigrated as fake. Such developments are distinctly damaging to the democratic process.

It is notable that in societies where there are multiple reliable sources of news (e.g. via quality newspapers and/or broadcasters), the tendency for social media to generate tight echo chambers is diluted.[7] In short, the arrival of social media, far from making the BBC anachronistic, makes it ever more required!

What we take for granted

When you look out of the window, what do you see - buildings, cars, people, trees? What you do *not* see is the glass! Think for a moment about how it was to live before the invention of glass.

What is the "glass" for much of the contemporary western world? It is the Rule of Law and the set of institutions, ideas and values handed down from the Age of Enlightenment and the Scientific Revolution. These are the ideas that replaced superstition with science, dogma with reason, and fate with free will.

In the UK, these ideas and their associated values are embedded within public service broadcasting, with the BBC at its core. With its trusted news, its extensive coverage of public affairs, its commitment to impartiality, and its high quality programmes, the BBC has created an ecology of UK broadcasting which has enhanced us all as citizens.

Why we need the BBC

The case for the BBC follows from naturally from its role – that of a public broadcaster serving citizens. To fulfil this role, it must be universally available and free at the point of use. Any form of subscription model goes out of the window, being wrong in principle.

In order to maximise public value, the BBC must deliver programmes that appeal substantially *and* widely[8] and it must be accountable to the public.

---

[7] Dubois, E, and G Blank. (2018)

In contrast, advertising-driven private broadcasters primarily concerned with audience size are answerable only to their shareholders. If there is money to be made, the private sector is under pressure to go as far as the law allows. We know that hate-speech kills. Yet, in the USA, an ABC radio producer stated that "Our advertisers are aware that hate sells their products" (Williams, 1996;92).

Despite all the criticisms, the BBC remains not only the most trusted of all broadcasters, but also has higher trust ratings than quality newspapers, much higher ones than tabloids and multiple times higher than politicians.[9] Under pressure for good information during Covid, the public turned to the BBC, its website visits doubling within weeks.[10]

The BBC is a global success story and a hugely positive influence domestically. One reason for the success of the UK's creative industries lies in the high quality professional environment that the BBC creates and encourages, not just by its presence but also via the people it trains. With Government particularly keen for UK Ltd to succeed outside the EU, it seems the height of stupidity to attack a British success story which helps promote so much other success around it.

The Wider Political Context

One does not need to be a conspiracist to see that there is another agenda. Many have commented on the behaviour of the Johnson/Cummings government. The list is long: illegally advising the Queen to prorogue Parliament; the removal of senior civil servants; the promotion of unelected and unaccountable Special Advisers; the removal of the Whip from senior members of the Conservative Party; the setting up of a Commission to inquire into appointments to the judiciary; on and on we go. All the normal forms of checks and balance that have been a part of the British constitution are being removed one by one so that the Executive remains accountable only to itself – not to Parliament, not to the law, and certainly not to a public service broadcaster called the BBC.

Conclusions

The BBC must respond to its "friendly critics". This can be done with internal reform. Externally, there is a major fight ahead. As I write, the

---

[8] Technically, the area under the demand curve.
[9] Reuters, DNR, 2020
[10] Reuters, DNR, 2020

former Murdoch employee, Andrew Neil, is set to lead a right-wing, opinionated news channel. In today's post-truth world and with the UK ever more polarised, the UK needs more of the BBC, not more of Murdoch. Above all, we all need to realise, before it is too late, that the BBC is essential to our democracy.

About the Contributor

Dr Andrew Graham is a Trustee of the Europaeum (where, as Executive Chair until 1 October, 2020, he initiated a new Scholarship across 17 leading European universities), Founder and Senior Fellow of the Oxford Internet Institute and a Trustee of Reprieve. Previous positions include Master of Balliol College, Oxford, non-Executive Director of Channel 4 Television, Director of the Scott Trust, Acting Warden of Rhodes House, Rhodes Trustee, Fellow and Tutor in Economics at Balliol, and Economic Adviser to the Rt Hon John Smith (Leader of the Opposition) and Prime Minister, Harold Wilson. He has written widely on public service broadcasting (Graham and Davies 1990, 1997; Graham 1998, 2005, 2013).

Bibliography

CIGI-Ipsos (2019) https://www.cigionline.org/internet-survey-2019?gclid=EAIaIQobChMI-bGN2vzT5wIVyLTtCh1gAQc3EAAYASAAEgJyyPD_BwE (accessed 26/09/2020)

Dubois, E, and G Blank. 2018. "The Echo Chamber Is Overstated: the Moderating Effect of Political Interest and Diverse Media." Information Communication and Society 21 (5): 729–45.

Graham, A. and G. Davies (1990) Why Private Choice Needs Public Broadcasting Royal Television Society, London

Graham, A. and G. Davies (1997) Broadcasting, Society and Policy in the Multimedia Age John Libbey Media

Graham, A. (1998) "Broadcasting Policy and the Digital Revolution" in Jean Seaton (ed.) Politics and the Media: Harlots and Prerogatives at the Turn of the Millenium Blackwell Publishers

Graham, A. (2005) "It's the Ecology, Stupid" in Dieter Helm (ed.) Can the Market Deliver: Funding Public Service Television in the Digital Age John Libbey Publishing

Graham, A. (2013) "Is there still a place for Public Service Television?" in Robert G Picard and Paolo Sicialani (eds.) Effects of the Changing Economics of Broadcasting Reuters Institute for Journalism and the BBC Trust

Pentland, A. (2014) Social Physics: How Good Ideas Spread-The Lessons from a New Science Penguin Press

Reuters (2020) Digital News Report 2020 Reuters Institute, University of Oxford (pdf download)

Syed, M. (2019) Rebel Ideas: The Power of Diverse Thinking John Murray Press
Voice of the Listener and Viewer (2019) Response to the BBC Consultation: Age-related TV Licence Policy (pdf download)

Williams, R. (1996) Normal Service won't be Resumed: the future of public broadcasting Allen and Unwin Pty Ltd Australia

Chapter 2

Why I Hate the Beeb – Dominic Cummings in His Own Words

Professor Ivor Gaber brushes off the dust from some very old web postings by the Prime Minister's chief adviser and discovers that his enmity towards the BBC runs deep.

A long time ago (2004 to be precise) in a galaxy far away (but not that far away) a young right-winger established a think tank (as almost everyone was doing at the time). The right-winger was called Dominic Cummings and the short-lived thinktank was portentously titled the *New Frontiers Foundation.*

All of which might be little more than a tiny post script to the history of the rise of Boris Johnson and his entourage, but buried deep within the musty pages of deleted internet pages one finds an insight into how Cummings, the most powerful man in Downing Street, notwithstanding the PM, has been plotting against the BBC for the past 16 years at least. [11]

Robin Aitken, a former BBC reporter who has now morphed into one of its most virulent right-wing critics, in a *Daily Telegraph* article headlined "Dominic Cummings's blood feud with the BBC" described Cummings as "the BBC's single most dangerous opponent because he is one of the very few people on the Right who clearly understands that the BBC presents an obstacle to everything that Conservatives believe in. "[12] (See Aitken Chapter 12)

The prelude

Cummings begins articulating his rage about the BBC in January 2004 when he unambiguously describes it as "the mortal enemy" of the

---

[11]Rowena Mason (2020) 'Dominic Cummings thinktank called for 'end of BBC in current form' *The Guardian* 21 Jan 2020

[12]Robin Aitken (2020) 'Dominic Cummings's blood feud with the BBC is not over yet' *Daily Telegraph* 30 May 2020

Conservative Party. He is silent on the topic until July of that year. Perhaps the enlargement of the hated EU two months previously prompted that July post when, in considering issues such as the EU, the role of markets and even the non-existent weapons of mass destruction in Iraq, he observes: "The BBC is dominated by a culture that regards differing points of view … as immoral" and he goes on to say: "The privileged closed world of the BBC needs to be turned upside down and its very existence should be the subject of a very intense and well-funded campaign. ". To that end, unconcerned about being seen as "immoral" himself, he calls for "whistle blowers armed with internal memos and taped conversations of meetings. " to come forward and denounce the Corporation. A day later he adds, as an afterthought, that the Right should be campaigning for the legalisation of political advertising on television – presumably in the interests of balance. [13]

A Cummings plan.

By September of that year Cummings has sufficiently marshalled his anti-BBC argument into a plan of action for the Right consisting of: " 1) the undermining of the BBC's credibility; 2) the creation of a *Fox News* equivalent / talk radio shows / bloggers etc to shift the centre of gravity; 3) the end of the ban on TV political advertising. ". He recognises that these are rather ambitious long-term goals (though sixteen years later the prospects are looking decidedly rosy) but suggests that, in the interim, the Right should develop online networks: "scrutinising the BBC and providing information to commercial rivals with an interest in undermining the BBC's credibility. "

There is a certain amount of naivety here in the suggestion that *ITV or Channel Four* or *Channel 5* would have had any interest in seeking to undermine what they would then, and still do, see as their public service broadcasting partner.

In 2004 Cummings was prescient in talking about the need for scrutinising the BBC's reporting of any EU Referendum, saying their coverage must be "taken apart minute-by-minute", He applies the same judgement in the lead-up to the 2005 General Election urging on the Right which he says "must fire missile after missile at the BBC" - the long-term aim being to undermine the BBC's reputation "in the way *CBS'* reputation is being undermined now [in 2005]"

---

[13]Mason Op Cit

Cummings' blog for the *New Frontiers Foundation* ceased in 2004 and the organisation itself was dissolved two years later. When he resumed blogging duties in 2013 his antipathy to the BBC appears to have momentarily softened. In May 2014 he actually quotes the BBC in support of a battle he was waging with Nick Clegg "proving that I am telling the truth and Clegg is lying. ". Indeed, in August of the same year, he goes further, actually praising a BBC programme on genetics as "excellent". But, as far as praising the BBC is concerned, that's as good as it gets.

Take back control...of the BBC?

In June 2015 he's back on firmer ground when a new EU Referendum hove into view and, following the Tories' success in the May General Election, he writes: "Many in the BBC see the EU debate, as they saw the Euro debate, simply as 'internationalists v racists' which makes them even less inclined to challenge people like Ken Clarke who is routinely allowed to make factually wrong assertions without challenge on the *Today* programme. "

In 2017 the *Spectator* magazine published Cummings' account of the Brexit campaign. In this lengthy blog he repeatedly refers to BBC staff as being out-of-touch and elite - a theme that has obsessed him ever since his time as Campaign Director of '*Business for Sterling*' which was formed to campaign against the UK joining the Euro. In his Brexit blog he recalls: ". . one famous BBC correspondent said to us during the Euro battle 'The thing is we [the BBC] like cappuccinos and hate racists. ' Such feelings tend to overwhelm reason and leave people blind to things that ought to be obvious"

In a later post Cummings suggests: "They [BBC journalists] have little or no idea what it's like to struggle on £18,000 a year in a part of Birmingham that has been radically changed by immigration in a short period knowing one has no reserves to call on. " and he goes on: "The BBC and other influential institutions are dominated by such people so it is almost inevitable that they see issues like the EU in ways that seem distorted to others".

Warming to his theme,Cummings concludes: "Another feature of richer people in my experience is that they tend to think that their greater wealth is a consequence of their virtues – they don't seem to reflect much on the genetic roll of the dice. " (One notes in passing that Cummings, educated privately and at Oxford, married to the daughter of a Baronet, didn't do so badly when those same dice rolled for him)[14].

Cummings is equally scathing about how BBC producers were covering the Referendum. He outlines an occasion when the Leave campaign was launching a report that claimed that leaving the EU would be economically advantageous for the UK. He quotes an unnamed BBC TV producer who, Cummings claimed, evinced a lack of interest in the story saying: "sounds boring...Who's fronting it? Got any new names? Any chance of Boris putting the boot into Dave and George?". Notwithstanding, Cummings is not shy in taking credit for manipulating the media: "It was not in our power to change basics of how the media works. We therefore twisted them to our advantage to hack the system. "

Managing/massaging the media?

No matter how much he despised the BBC Cummings recognised its importance, noting how Boris Johnson's telegenic personality ensured that it was the Cummings-led Leave campaign, rather than the one led by Nigel Farage, that received maximum media exposure in the Referendum, and, in so doing, he suggests, secured the additional votes that he believed achieved the victory: "Without Boris" he wrote "Farage would have been a much more prominent face on TV during the crucial final weeks, probably the most prominent face. (We had to use Boris as leverage with the BBC to keep Farage off and even then they nearly screwed us as ITV did. It is extremely plausible that this would have lost us over 600,000 vital middle-class votes. "[15]

It's illuminating to be able now to look back to 2004 when that little-known director of a short-lived right-wing 'think thank' mused on the BBC - his "mortal enemy" - and suggested that the Corporation should be undermined to the extent that its very existence should be questioned. In 2020 Cummings can regard the present moves to de-criminalise non-payment of the BBC licence fee (bringing huge financial implications for the BBC's income) with some satisfaction. And, with a review of the BBC's Charter due in 2027 Cummings can look forward to seeing his campaign to undermine the BBC succeeding, not in one grand swoop, as maybe he hoped, but in a virtual death by a thousand cuts.

---

[14]Wikipedia (2020) 'Dominic Cummings' https://en. wikipedia. org/wiki/Dominic Cummings accessed 19 September 2020

[15.] Dominic Cummings (2017) 'How the Brexit referendum was won' The Spectator 9 January 2017 https://www. spectator. co. uk/article/dominic-cummings-how-the-brexit-referendum-was-won accessed 19 September 2020

About the author:

Ivor Gaber is Professor of Political Journalism at the University of Sussex who was an independent editorial adviser to the BBC and a former broadcast journalist with BBC Radio and TV, ITV News, Channel Four News and Sky News.

Chapter 3

The BBC And Its Bias – Go Woke Go Broke. It Is The Un-Knowing Which Is The Problem.

Rod Liddle is an enigma. A former editor of the flagship BBC Radio Four 'Today' programme, he is now a columnist for the Sunday Times, Spectator and the Sun! Rod is now firmly outside the Beeb tent urinating in.

One of my favourite moments of television viewing in this strange and dark year was the outgoing Director General of the BBC, Tony Hall, explaining why the corporation had decided to drop the singing of Rule Britannia and Land of Hope and Glory from the Last Night of the Proms. The BBC had already, needlessly, dug itself a capacious hole and Tony had turned up with a big spade to continue the work. It was purely for "artistic reasons", his emollience announced, his nose growing fractionally longer with every second of the interview.

Earlier the BBC had – shamefully, out of cowardice – attempted to suggest via a briefing that the guest conductor, the Ukrainian-Finnish Dalia Stasevska, being a bit of a Leftie, had objected to the jingoistic nature of the words of those anthems. Vilified on social media as the furore grew, poor Ms Stasevska felt obliged to release a statement saying that she had made no such objections and that it would have been "arrogant" to do so. Indeed. Who, exactly, would have had such arrogance? Only the BBC. It cannot stand Last Night of the Proms – all that flag waving and patriotism – which is why the programme has been made more (here's the word they cower behind) "diverse" over the last decade.

Much as it cannot stand Jeremy Clarkson, Andrew Neil, Brexit, the Conservative Party or a white male Time Lord, It took the decision to infuriate a large proportion of its audience because it inhabits a woke echo chamber where almost everybody has the same fashionable opinions, buttressed by their hugely unrepresentative followers on social media. The producers and presenters do not think that binning Land of Hope and Glory is a political act at all, simply that it is "right". And this is the problem which Tim Davie faces: not so much that the BBC is institutionally biased towards a liberal leftish position on almost every issue, a bias which shows through in every area of its output – news, documentaries, drama and most obviously comedy – but that the staff do not feel it is a bias at all, simply decency and that beyond W1 everyone shares their opinions. But they do not. Far from it.

Hang up your opinions on an old coat peg (if you can find one.)

In that same interview, Lord Hall remarked on the question of political bias that staff were expected to hang up their opinions on a coat peg when they entered Broadcasting House. Leaving aside the issue as to where one might find a coat peg large enough to accommodate Emily Maitlis's array of raiment, this facile observation revealed a patent lack of understanding of the BBC's psychology. I repeat: they do not think they are opinions at all, simply that they are right. And there is uniformity of opinion among the largely young, largely arts or social science grad, largely metropolitan, exclusively middle class liberals who work for the organisation. Let me give you a couple of examples.

The BBC news programmes have a copious data base of potential contributors. On at least one programme contributors who can be relied upon to oppose untrammelled immigration, or doubt that our society is corrupted by structural racism, or have misgivings about the transgender agenda, are known as "Dial A C**t". The problem here is that – depending upon which polls you believe – between sixty per cent and eighty per cent of the population think immigration should be either reduced or stopped. They are all c**ts, then, those people. The same c**ts who sing Land of Hope and Glory and voted for Brexit: a majority of the population, a majority of licence fee payers. C**ts the lot of them.

Probably the same people who objected to the BBC shoe-horning an anti-Brexit theme into Dr Who. Or there's this. Twenty years ago, when I was editor of the Today programme, I took to the Controller of Editorial Policy a series of complaints from Eurosceptic politicians to the effect that our coverage grossly under-represented the Eurosceptic cause. "What you have to understand, Rod," I was told, "is that these people are all mad." And yet even then, two decades ago, those views had considerable purchase – beyond the north circular.

BBC bias in the blood? Does it need a 'reality check'?

That the BBC is biased seems to me a statement so incontestable that it would be otiose to run through the evidence. The myriad of independent reports – such as the Wilson Report from 2005 (i)which concluded the BBC was deeply partisan over Europe even if it did not think it was, or the Institute for Economic Affairs report (2017)(ii)which showed that panellists on both Question Time and Any Questions were 68 per cent in favour of Remain. (This last survey, incidentally, followed an open letter from MPs complaining about "pessimistic and skewed" coverage of Brexit) I could go on and on. We have long since passed the time when it was acceptable for the BBC to shrug off these observations with the banal rejoinder, trotted out once again by that political titan Gary Lineker in September 2020: "The left thinks the BBC is biased against them and so does the right – so maybe we're neutral." (iii)

Incidentally, I have no doubt that the BBC, in general, found Jeremy Corbyn hard to stomach. The bias is more cultural than political. It's not necessarily pro-Labour.

There is a certain naivety at the heart of this problem, rooted in that notion advanced by Tony Hall that one might shed oneself of political opinions whilst at work, and then presumably resume them once you've clocked off. The same naivety which resulted in the creation of the BBC's "Reality Check", headed by the journalist Chris Morris. The idea of Reality Check was that Chris and his small team would wander along after a disputatious argument between politicians to adjudicate who was telling the truth, that is they would give the "facts". The trouble was, whose facts? As was demonstrated in an acrimonious interview between Morris and the former Conservative minister Peter Lilley, Morris was not providing "facts" – simply countering Lilley's opinions with opinions of his own drawn from reports which Morris found agreeable.

Beyond that, though, the idea that in this complex, fissiparous, world Chris Morris and his team alone have the sole access to the "truth" on every possible topic is so naïve as to be laughable. I might point out too that Mr Reality Checker was responsible for a five part radio series, "Brexit: A Guide for the Perplexed". He used a total of 24 main interviews for this unbiased, unpartisan revelation of the truth – of which 18 were speaking from a Remain perspective. Only seven per cent of the words uttered throughout the series were spoken by people who were in favour of what the majority wanted to do – leave the European Union. (iv)

The unknowing known

But still, the problem is less in the bias than in the un-knowing. The arrogant conviction that it is not bias at all. The aforementioned Newsnight presenter, Emily Maitlis, has twice been reprimanded by her employers for allowing her own political opinions to either distort an interview or indeed make a party political broadcast against the government at the start of the programme. But there is not the slightest evidence that either she, or her editor Esme Wren, think she has done anything wrong at all. And there is seemingly nobody on that benighted show to offer a word of dissent, to dispute or contradict Maitlis's inane bien pensant opinions. They are all agreed that they are not opinions at all, just fact.

Comfortably cocooned in its 'right-on ' bubble, the BBC has long since lost touch with the mores and cultural values of the mass of people who pay for its existence. This is more of a crisis, I would suggest, than the diminishing interest young people show in the BBC (despite the Corporation's continual obeisance to this minority sector of the population). Yet all that is needed is a certain awareness, an honesty and a stripping away of that certitude which seems to afflict the liberal left. An understanding that what they think are facts are really just opinions.

Hope and Glory for the BBC?

Tim Davie's first act as incoming Director General was to restore the singing of those two jingoistic anthems in Last Night of the Proms. Wasn't that hard to do, was it? The finale was conducted with bravura by Dalia Stasevska, whose face, at the end, was suffused with jubilation and delight. Everybody happy.

If Davie can continue to tilt the Corporation towards those values and aspirations shared by the majority of British people, then perhaps old 'Auntie' still has a future. But the rot runs terribly deep and they do not think it is rot at all.

About the Contributor

Rod Liddle is one of Britain's leading columnists. He treads the boards weekly in The Sunday Times, The Spectator and The Sun. In a previous life he was the Editor of the Today programme on BBC Radio Four.

References

http://downloads.bbc.co.uk/bbctrust/assets/files/pdf/our_work/govs/independentpanelreport.pdf

https://iea.org.uk/media/iea-analysis-shows-systemic-bias-against-leave-supporters-on-flagship-bbc-political-programmes/

https://www.thetimes.co.uk/article/gary-lineker-interview-the-bbc-never-asked-me-to-tone-down-tweets-they-trust-me-sxcw0hprm

http://news-watch.co.uk/wp-content/uploads/2018/04/news-watch-survey-of-radio-4s-brexit-a-guide-for-the-perplexed.pdf

Chapter 4

Tim Davie-Putting Some Old Spice into the 'Auntie' BBC Brand

The new Director General had a life before the BBC. He worked in marketing household name consumer goods in Britain and the USA. What transferable skills does he bring to the BBC 'Brand'? is the question John Mair addresses.

Many Cambridge English graduates try to go off to the media world, even to the top places like the BBC. Not for Tim Davie. Forget Beowulf, he went off to be a brand manager at the University of FMCG (Fast Moving Consumer Goods) Procter and Gamble. They sell huge consumer lines like *Tide, Ariel ,Head and Shoulders*, *Vick* and men's toiletries like *Old Spice* which is the brand one can assume the young Davie managed.

Procter and Gamble was, even when he joined in 1991, emblematic in marketing history. Started small in the USA a hundred years before, it was now worldwide with tentacles everywhere. It was the world's biggest advertiser and had got mass marketing down to a tee.

The company and the company men/women had/have an almost quasi-religious belief in their purpose in life. Very American. The company motto speaks volumes *'Touching Lives, Improving Life'*. Davie the Whitgift School scholarship boy topped up by Selwyn College Cambridge could not hope for a better training in the arts and science of marketing ,unless of course he had joined the other multi-national FMCG behemoth Unilever.

What is a brand manager?

But just what does a brand manager do? He/she is a baron in the kingdom of the whole company. He/she 'owns' the brand for a time. He/she rules the brand-the marketing, the positioning in the market, the market research commissioned, the advertising, the special offers everything but the composition and manufacture of the product. That is fixed in the short term. Some may even choose to extend the brand to new variants and new niches which *Old Spice* has done since Tim left P&G.

The brand manager will watch market share data with an eagle eye. They will know whom their direct competitors are on the supermarket shelves. Usually they are from Unilever. For every *Tide* a *Persil* , for every *Crest* toothpaste a *Gibbs SR*.

The new brand manager inherits the good and the bad legacies of those who went before. You live or you die the brand for your time in charge. It is a brutal ride, do well and you go up. Do less well and you're out or to a brand in corporate Siberia. Tim went up and out to *Pepsi*.

The company corporately too is brutal .Today they market just 63 Procter and Gamble brands worldwide .*Old Spice* is still there. Their portfolio of brands simply got too big and too wide so in 2015 P&G decided to slew off ballast of 100 brands by selling them to others.

P&G Values.

The company, it is American, is strong in its 'mission'. Being good is a corporate must. Today it is Climate Change, tomorrow who knows? P&G is strong on value and ethics. Some of them can be read across to the BBC.

On integrity the P&G way-always try to the right thing, be honest and straightforward with each other, operate within the letter and spirit of the law, uphold the values and principles of the company and base decisions on data and calculate the risk before making it.

In the BBC, that simple list would take a plethora of committees drafting and redrafting. Lots of people with fancy titles to finesse it-CEP(Controller Editorial Policy),CPA (Chief Political Adviser) etc, .They like titles, they like committees. Producer and editorial guidelines would be churned out, destroying forests in the process. In essence, P&G teaches its people to be straight and honest in their dealings with customers and others. That should go over every door in every BBC building in the land.

Likewise on trust: for P&G -respect colleagues, customers and consumers, have confidence in capabilities and intention, and people work best where there is a foundation of trust

In BBC speak, know and respect your audience, over estimate their understanding of the product/programmes and give colleagues a sound foundation of trust. None of that is the science of propulsion but in the dog eat dog world in the Corporation, 'Ethics' may just be seen as a County close to London. It should not be.

A Passion for Winning

The passion to be number one is in the core values-determined to be the best at doing what matters most, a healthy dissatisfaction with the status quo and have a compelling desire to improve and to win in the marketplace.

The BBC having been a television monopoly for half a century has found itself in a very crowded market for eyeballs for the second near fifty. Since the 'streamers'- *Netflix, Amazon, Disney* + for example came ashore in the UK many viewers have flooded to subscription. But 'Auntie' has lifted up her skirts and produced the popular like *'Strictly Come Dancing'* and other hits to compete.

Itchy feet

After two years in the powerhouse of P&G , Tim went off to another American (essentially marketing)operation-*Pepsi Cola*. Always number two in the cola marketplace throughout the world .The nice guys were not winning.

Pepsi UK needed a marketing manager with ideas and pizazz to get ink and image. Tim provided that by painting a Concorde in *Pepsi* colours and getting an entire edition of the *Daily Mirror* (then a huge selling newspaper)wrap around in *Pepsi* colours. Plainly the P&G training had served him well. He mounted the *Pepsi* marketing ladder swiftly in the UK and the USA to end up as the Vice President for Marketing and Franchise twelve years later.

Joining 'Auntie'

Then to the clutches of the BBC in 2005 .He was Director General's Mark Thompson's first big external appointment as the Director of Marketing and Communications. From FMCG to programmes audiences and image. A big jump one might imagine .The BBC like *Old Spice* and *Pepsi* a heritage product but one with a very different pedigree and a very different history. 'Marketing' was (and maybe still is) not a term of endearment in the Corporation. Producers had ideas, they made programmes, maybe people listened and watched. Genius and serendipity ruled.

How did Tim do in moving that super-tanker round? Did Tim manage to reposition the Corporation, tie it in with core customers and protect the brand values in his short time in that post? Plainly his bosses were pleased.

He stayed in that Marketing job just three years before persuading DG Mark Thompson that his future was on another branch of the BBC executive ladder-Programme Management. He became head of audio and music-in effect Director of Radio in 2008. He later told me that he loved the job.

Wireless supremo

In that role he could at last use the words of the bard rather than the brand. Tim succeeded well ,popular amongst staff(unusual in the BBC) until he was forced to step in as the 'Supply DG' after George Entwistle's disastrous 54 day reign in 2012. Then to head *BBC Worldwide* and *BBC Studios* to make serious revenue - £1.2 b in 2019 – to put on the BBC screens for British licence payers and others worldwide. The deal maker in the brand manager came out in him.

Editor in Chief and Marketeer in chief.

Now that Tim is not just Director General but the overall marketing director of the Corporation, the major strategy decisions are all his to call.

There are plenty to fill his in-tray and exercise his marketing brain. Is the BBC a tired and withering brand-what can be done about that? Is there a very threat to its existence in the increasingly shrill noises coming out of Downing street about 'whacking it' ? And what about imposing a Chairman who does not share the core values of the Corporation? Will the BBC find new niches-podcasting already up and running. What next? Will it shrink to fit the new reality of the broadcasting market place? Will the BBC brand wither under his control? Will it thrive? Will it find new niches?

Even more marketing/political/business challenges face the BBC ....How will it differentiate itself as brand leader from the new kids on the block-mainly American streaming companies? How do you monetise the BBC brand to make up for lost revenue without the customers/licence payers noticing? How do you act to stop the customers not paying for the product especially once non-payment of the licence fee is decriminalised?

Tim Davie is in charge now of one of the biggest and best respected brands in the world-the BBC. It is a national and international treasure. The huge challenge now is to keep that brand fresh or just merely alive. As DG Davie will need all the marketing skills acquired at *P&G* and *Pepsi* to rise to the challenge of 'saving' the BBC.

About the Contributor

John Mair is a former BBC producer. In a previous life he worked in marketing and market research for Unilever for two years. He has edited 37 'hackademic' books in the last decade. This is the latest.

Reference

P&G company website .https://www.pg.co.uk/.url Accessed October 1st 2020

Chapter 5

Letter to the Director General

Raymond Snoddy has been watching and reporting on the BBC for nearly half a century. He has been the Media Editor of the Times and of the Financial Times. He sends a letter from Ruislip to the very new Director General.

September 2020

Dear Tim,

I was reluctant to get in touch with you earlier because you obviously needed a little time to settle in as the 17th director-general of the BBC.

Also it's far from clear that you are in need of any advice from a journalist parked for many years on the side lines. You have been at the BBC since 2005 and even got the whiff of a genuine BBC scandal as acting Director-General in the wake of the *Newsnight* –Lord McAlpine "story" and the abrupt departure of George Entwistle as DG after 54 days..

You are probably already wading knee-deep in advice, strategy reports, the latest public opinion surveys, and unless the BBC has changed faster than appears to be the case, there will be consultants beavering away on the future of public service broadcasting somewhere in the background.

However given that I have been watching the affairs of the BBC since well before you joined Procter & Gamble as a trainee in 1991 straight out of university, it might just be possible to make a few helpful observations.

First a very old joke – apologies in advance- involving a naïve Englishman asking for directions in Ireland who received the wise reply: " I wouldn't start from here if I was you."

If only you could start from a different place but alas you are stuck with an unparalleled collection of interlocking problems the like of which no BBC director-general has ever had to face before.

The only thing missing at the moment is a war.

Recent DG's, almost without exception, have faced unrelenting criticism and scandals of a political, sexual or journalistic nature – controversies that brought down two director-generals, Alasdair Milne and Greg Dyke, before Entwistle's uber short reign.

Usually the rows came one at a time although running through the recent history of British broadcasting there has always been the leitmotif of Right-wing press opposition most notably in the efforts by different generations of Murdochs to agitate for a much smaller BBC,as indeed they still are.

All your troubles..

Unfortunately Tim you seem to be facing simultaneous waves of troubles and at least no-one can doubt your courage in taking on the job in the first place.

All you have to do is cope with:

- A Government that makes no secret of its hostility to the BBC, apparently hell-bent on decriminalising the licence fee and with it undermining the very idea of a national public service broadcaster.
  Things are very likely to get worse when Sir David Clementi stands down as your chairman next February. You can expect a hostile replacement with Lord Moore former editor of the *Daily Telegraph* being tipped for the job. Lord Moore is a well known opponent of both the BBC and its licence fee and was even fined for refusing to pay the licence fee because he disapproved of a BBC programme
- Deep fissures in society from Brexit and Leave, from North and South, Rich and Poor and the centrifugal forces that could yet tear the UK apart. In such a world the BBC's version of "due impartiality" appears increasingly to satisfy very few
- Then there are the social and economic impact of the worst Pandemic since the Spanish flu of 1918-just four years before the BBC was founded.
- And as you said, the decision to make most over 75-year-olds pay the full licence fee again is not the best of looks even if you inherited it from your immediate processor Tony Hall who in turn acted under huge political duress
- The greatest long-term threat of all comes from the march of the streamers such as *Netflix, Apple, Disney* and *Amazon* and many more besides. It has led many to view broadcasting as a mere transaction – I

pay a subscription for what I want and only what I want - rather than a cultural good that helps to define a society and indeed democracy itself

- **B**ubbling along there are still the many unresolved issues involving diversity, inclusivity, gender equality and the long promised hope of finally doing something about excessive bureaucracy. There are other issues but that's probably enough to be getting on with for now. Together they add to up an existential threat to the BBC as it is currently constituted.

Last hooray for Britannia and for humour?

At least Tim you started well by overturning the ridiculous decision to ban the choral rendition of *Rule Britannia* from the last night of the Proms. Few believed that the decision has been taken for artistic reasons as claimed rather than a confused "woke" brew of *Black Lives Matter* combined with the ahistorical mixture of upending slavery-tainted statues and ghosts from the past. You were also right to warn BBC journalists that if they wanted to become controversial commentators that was fine, but they shouldn't do it while working at the BBC.

Less certain was your comment about cracking down on left-wing comedy. All comedy, or more precisely satire, tends to mock those in authority and there are sound reasons why the Conservatives, who have been in power in one shape or another for more than a decade, should be the butt of many jokes.

What can you do?

So what Tim, given the extremely limited room for manoeuvre, can now be done?

Your hand is not completely empty of cards. As deputy chairman of Hammersmith and Fulham Conservative Party in the 1990s it's quite difficult for the Government to portray you as a 'left-wing agitator'.

By general consent the BBC acquitted itself well during the early months of the Pandemic producing essential educational materials for locked down schoolchildren and providing vital information for the nation.

Overall the Corporation managed to breathe new life into its' traditional role as a national public service broadcaster.

Surely the Boris Johnson Government would not stage a full-frontal attack on the BBC, however much it would like to do so, in the midst of a Covid-19/ Brexit perfect storm?

Probably not, except there is a residual danger that the Government might be happy for a populist distraction from current harsh realities and criticisms such as decriminalisation as a prelude to a final abolition of the licence once the BBC's centenary year of 2022 is safely out of the way.

Fight clever? Fight long.

Because you face multiple threats your response is going to have to be multi-dimensional too, embracing challenges from the government, the licence payers and the BBC's staff.

The sharpest of all the battles is going to be with the Government because that is where the greatest antagonism lies, as does ultimately the money.

The BBC will have to try to convince the Government of the counter-productive nature of de-criminalisation of the licence fee without any accompanying compensation. The Corporation will also have to try to seek some compensation for the £150 million or so loss to the BBC arising from the provision of free licence fees to the over 75s on income support.

Given the depth of the Covid-19/Brexit recession and the scale of job losses and company collapses everywhere from hospitality and tourism to the aviation industries such pleas are likely to fall on deaf ears.

Your strategy has to be therefore to push for an independent inquiry into the future structure and financing of the BBC and the future importance of public service broadcasting.

This would have particular reference to the future of the licence fee, whether it will remain the least bad way of funding the Corporation beyond 2027 or whether there are better, and less controversial alternatives to funding a national public service broadcaster. It could also have a look at changing technologies and the increasing importance of the creative industries to the UK economy in future.

There has not been an independent look at the finances of the BBC since Prime Minister Margaret Thatcher asked the free market economist Sir Alan Peacock in 1986, when you were still in secondary school, to see whether advertising could replace the licence fee. Sir Alan came up with "wrong answer" and found it could not and in fact ended up strengthening the licence fee, although the Peacock Committee did recommended that pensioners on benefits should have free licence fees.

I need hardly point out how dramatic the changes in communications have been in the three decades and more since then.

Of course it is dangerous pinning your future on the uncertain outcome of a formal inquiry and the Government's reaction to it, but doing nothing and the status quo do not appear attractive options.

Or, death by a thousand cuts?

The worst outcome of all for the BBC and the country would be a piecemeal hacking at the institution starting with the deeply damaging decriminalising of the licence fee.

You are going to have to engage more directly with the BBC audience- the licence payers - to convince them of the value of what the BBC does and the wide range of services they pay for.

Making occasional set speeches at broadcasting industry conferences – there won't be conferences for ages anyway – simply won't hack it anymore.

Far too many people think the BBC is there just to provide entertainment and finds the Corporation wanting when compared with *Netflix*, without realising how false such a comparison is.

Selling the BBC to licence payers.

The BBC has for years been weak at explaining what the Corporation offers, everything from local, regional, national and international news, five television channels,ten radio channels,a leading website to five orchestras, world class broadcast engineering research and the wonderful BBC World Service.

Perhaps there should be a campaign using humour along the lines of *What Has The BBC Ever Done For You*? If it fails to reach all of the wider audience it might just reach MP's who appear to be sleep-walking into destroying an important UK institution.

More should also be done to explain what "due impartiality" means in an age of mendacious social media outlets and fake news.

It should not, however mean the automatic need to balance every statement with an equal and opposite response when the response is simply not true, however powerful a political mouth it emerges from.

BBC journalists have to be better prepared and informed so that statements that are manifestly untrue are fact-checked in as real time as possible.

Less means better?

Here I know I am pushing at an open door but with limited resources, that could become even less in future, the BBC will have to concentrate more on a fewer number of high impact programmes.

Forget the fact that newspapers will carp about the number of repeats, the notion of repeats has been superseded by the way we now view. There are no repeats in the land of the *iPlayer* and catch-up streaming, there are just programmes that you want to see for the first time whether it's months after first transmission or not.

De-layer. Now! At last.

Finally you have to be radical about culture, meetings and bureaucracy. Of course you will have to deal with making the BBC more representative of the country it serves both in terms of gender and ethnic diversity.

You might also sit down to watch again all three series of *W1A* where the satire often failed to keep up with the toe-curling BBC reality.

Every DG of recent times has promised to cut down persistent BBC bureaucracies. Why don't you be the one to actually do it?

Tim you should be a walking-talking BBC DG – Covid permitting - finding ideas for greater efficiency from the very best place to find them, on the shop floor from the people who really know.

Talent pays or pay talent?

You must also do something about stars' salaries. The public have not understood the concept that the BBC exists in a marketplace for talent or that in these difficult times for so many people the BBC bill for talent rose by £1 million to £144 million last year.

The truth is you might have to let some of the big names go if they will not accept salary cuts when their contracts run out. There are always talented young people looking for opportunities who will do the jobs for £250,000 rather than £500,000.

Bring on the women.

Almost finally, a small structural change might help because you have got such a big job to do. As a non-journalist why not appoint Fran Unsworth, BBC Director of News as a Deputy DG and Charlotte Moore, Director of

Content as another while continuing to do their existing jobs of course. It would ease the personal burden while promoting two women without paying a penny more.

But the most important thing I want to say Tim is that I thought you were the right person to be appointed to lead the BBC through these most difficult of times.

Go and prove me right.

Yours

Raymond Snoddy

West London

September 2020

Chapter 6

The BBC – Britishness, Broadcasting and the Culture Wars

War on three fronts faces the New DG. Culture War. Professor Leighton Andrews with a report from the battlefield.

There are certain regular events in the BBC's institutional calendar which give rise to questions about its role and value – the appointment of a new Director-General, or the Chair of whatever governing body runs the BBC, Charter Review and Licence Fee negotiations. Many of the questions raised at these junctures recur – the durability of the Licence Fee itself, the forms and substance of its accountability, the distinctiveness of the BBC's services, its impact (s) on the wider media market, how well its universality serves different audiences, its diversity, its efficiency or otherwise. The BBC has historically played such a significant role in shaping what it means to be British that it is inevitable and right that these issues should be up for near permanent debate.

The forces amass

Anyone who has worked for the Corporation will be used to reading headlines about 'the BBC's worst-ever week' or even forecast obituaries of '*the last days of th*e Beeb (Lipman 1986)

So are things different this time? Up to a point. There is a dangerous cocktail facing the new Director-General:

1. The impact of austerity cuts suffered from 2010
2. The potential decriminalisation of the licence fee
3. The drop in the number of licence fee-paying households
4. The rise of subscription-based streaming services
5. The launch of alternative news services on radio and television
6. A serious Conservative-led 'culture war' supported in Parliament and through social media

The BBC was forced to take its share of cuts in 2010. The result was responsibility for the funding of the *World Service*, and the bulk of *S4C's* funding, from within the Licence Fee, as well as the transfer of responsibility for funding free TV licences for older viewers and support for broadband rollout in 2015. A settlement of £253 million towards the free television licences for over-75s came from DWP in 2019-20, and the new scheme, due to start in June 2020, was deferred as a result of the coronavirus outbreak with the BBC absorbing the extra costs. The BBC had 31% less to spend than if the licence fee had risen with inflation since 2010 (BBC, 2020).

A Licence to lose money?

Decriminalisation of the Licence Fee is likely to cost the BBC £200 million (BBC, 2020). At the time of writing (29th September) the Government's decision in response to its consultation (DCMS, 2020) had not been announced, but decriminalisation has been extensively trailed.

The BBC reported 250,000 fewer licence fee payers year on year in its Annual Report. Licence Fee revenue was accordingly down by £170 million from 2018-19 (BBC, 2020).

Subscription-based services such as *Netflix* and *Amazon Prime* and *Disney+* are eating into the BBC's share of viewing time (OFCOM, 2020) and this has been accentuated during the pandemic.

New competitive news services are being developed in the UK, with active encouragement from the Government. *Times Radio* launched in June with the Prime Minister's 'first sit-down broadcast interview' since the start of the coronavirus lockdown (Ponsford, 2020). Andrew Neil has left the BBC to head *GB News*, backed by *Discovery*, which he has said will 'champion robust, balanced debate', and *News Corporation* is also said to be considering a similar move (Barker, 2020). Neil has said *GB News* will not be rolling news but opinionated news on the *MSNBC* or *Fox* models using 'anchors with a bit of edge, bit of attitude, bit of personality' (GMB, 2020).

War on the Culture Front.

All of that is the backdrop to a culture war, supported by key figures in the government, actively coordinated in Parliament and pressure groups outside, utilising social media. The three most powerful men in the government – Johnson, Gove and Cummings - have 'form' when it comes to the BBC.

The Prime Minister himself wrote in the past that 'the prevailing view of BBC newsrooms is, with honourable exceptions, statist, corporatist, defeatist, anti-business, Europhile and, above all, overwhelmingly biased to the Left'; he called for the next Director-General to be a Tory, saying 'if we can't change the Beeb, we can't change the country' (Johnson, 2012). Earlier he also said that he consumes 'vast quantities of news – but almost entirely without the assistance of the BBC. ' But he also denied he was 'some kind of Beeb-basher' and said 'it is a great national institution, and at its best the BBC sets standards for programmes of all kinds' (Johnson, 2010).

Nearly twenty years ago, former BBC *Today Programme* producer Michael Gove said that the BBC was 'a lumbering anachronism' and called for 'the abolition of the licence fee' and the privatisation of the BBC (Gove, 2001).

The Prime Minister's chief of staff Dominic Cummings used to run a think-tank, the *New Frontiers Foundation*, with James Frayne, a Conservative pollster and former Director of Policy and Strategy at *Policy Exchange*, another think-tank co-founded by Michael Gove which is close to Number 10. Frayne became director of communications at the Department for Education for a period during Michael Gove's term as Secretary of State. Cummings was Gove's SPAD (Special Adviser) at DFE. The *Guardian has* published a series of blogposts by the think-tank from 2004, which indicated the depth of Cummings' anguish about the BBC. These said that the BBC was the Conservative Party's 'mortal enemy' and called for:

1) The undermining of the BBC's credibility;
2) The creation of a Fox News equivalent / talk radio shows / bloggers etc to shift the centre of gravity
3) The end of the ban on TV political advertising' *(Guardian*, 2020). (**See** Ivor Gab**er Chapter 2)**

A trawl through Wayback Machine shows that the think tank had a lot to say about the BBC's 'pro-Europe' 'cultural bias' at the time, a view that was to a degree separately acknowledged in a report by the BBC Governors (BBC, 2005). Indeed, since the 2000s, BBC figures themselves, have recognised the dangers of the Corporation having a metropolitan liberal culture (Marr, 2004).

The *NFF* posts also include a clear statement that 'The Tories Must fight a Culture War' against the metropolitan elite, recognising that culture wars are not a short-term activity (NFF, 2004). The Conservative Party lacked a popular movement in the country to complement it. Well, today, that may have changed.

Culture Wars and the BBC are not new. Shortly after I was appointed as BBC Head of Public Affairs in 1993, but before I took up the job, I attended, with my then work colleague John Bercow, a lunch with Julian Lewis, founder of the *Media Monitoring Unit* which would scout out potential BBC bias. On that occasion, I recall he had a particular concern about BBC Drama. And then, we didn't have social media.

Reform the BBC in Three Easy Steps.

The three conditions that the Cummings-led think-tank set for tackling the BBC are being met. First, the undermining of the BBC. A populist campaign has been waged by the Blue Collar group of Conservative MPs against the BBC's proposals on TV licences for the over-75s, seeking to switch the blame for this decision from the Government to the BBC (Blue Collar Conservatism, 2020). They have also orchestrated a letter to the incoming Director-General, which asserts that the BBC is widely seen as 'anti-British' (Loder, 2020). Meanwhile, a well-funded *#DefundBBC* campaign in running on social media, backed by prominent Brexiteers outside Parliament (DefundBBC, 2020) supporting the decriminalisation of the Licence Fee.

The second of Cummings' objectives, the creation of *Fox News/Talk radio* equivalents is being established. The question that remains open is whether broadcasting legislation will be reviewed to change definitions of impartiality and bias and *OFCOM's* role in policing those.

In the third area, political advertising on television, it may now be that the advent of social media advertising, particularly on *Facebook* (Andrews, 2019), used so effectively by Cummings in the EU Referendum campaign (Cummings, 2017) has made that less of a priority.

BBC fighting back!

Having said all of that, the BBC proved its worth to the government in the coronavirus crisis. BBC news services were the most-used sources of news and information about the Pandemic, and 80% of people trusted them. Over 14 million watched the Prime Minister's lockdown broadcast on the BBC on 23rd March, and 18. 7 million watched his lockdown-loosening broadcast on 10th May on BBC One (OFCOM, 2020). The BBC, like the Labour Party, is 'under new leadership', and whoever becomes its Chair –

TV Licence Fee Refusenik Charles Moore or anyone else - is unlikely to want to be the person who closes the Corporation down.

So the real threat to the BBC is not extinction, but a potential withering of services, more competition, and a reduced funding base. The likelihood is that Johnson will want to keep the BBC, but neuter it. Tim Davie in his first speech to staff (Davie, 2020) said this was the end of the BBC's 'linear expansion'. He is not the first Director-General to talk about the BBC doing more with less. Mark Thompson explicitly wrote into *Building Public Value* in 2004 that 'the BBC should be as small as its mission allows' (BBC, 2004). The immediate challenge for Davie is going to be delivering universalism and distinctiveness on a tighter budget – but in the pandemic, the BBC is proving its public value.

It will need to marshal its friends to win this war.

About the Contributor

Leighton Andrews is Professor of Public Service Leadership at Cardiff Business School. He was Minister for Education and Skills and Minister for Public Services in the Welsh Government between 2009-2016. He is the author of Facebook, the Media and Democracy (Routledge, 2019). He was the BBC's Head of Public Affairs from 1993-6.

References

Andrews, L. 2019. Facebook, the Media and Democracy (Routledge).

BBC, 2004. Building Public Value. https://downloads. bbc. co. uk/aboutthebbc/policies/pdf/bpv. pdf

BBC, 2005. BBC News coverage of the European Union – statement by the BBC Board of Governors, January 27th. http://www. bbc. co. uk/pressoffice/pressreleases/stories/2005/01_january/27/governors. shtml

BBC, 2020. Annual Report and Accounts. BBC. 15th September. http://downloads. bbc. co. uk/aboutthebbc/reports/annualreport/2019-20. pdf

Blue Collar Conservativism, 2020. BBC Fails to Correct Course. 26th July. https://www. bluecollarconservatism. co. uk/media

Cummings, D. 2017. **On** the referendum #22: Some basic numbers for the Vote Leave campaign 30th January. https://dominiccummings. files. wordpress. com/2017/01/20170130-referendum-22-numbers. pdf

Davie, T. 2020. Tim Davie's Introductory speech as BBC Director-General. BBC Media Centre, 3rd September. https://www. bbc. co. uk/mediacentre/speeches/2020/tim-davie-intro-speech

DCMS, 2020. Consultation on decriminalising TV Licence Evasion. . Department of Culture, Media and Sport, 5th February. https://www. gov. uk/government/consultations/consultation-on-decriminalising-tv-licence-evasion

DefundBBC, 2020. Tired of paying for BBC waste and bias? DefundBBC. https://www. defundbbc. uk

Guardian, 2020. 'Mortal enemy': what Cummings' Thinktank said about the BBC. Guardian. 21st January. https://www. theguardian. com/politics/2020/jan/21/mortal-enemy-what-cummings-thinktank-said-about-bbc

GMB, 2020. Anchors with a bit of edge, bit of attitude, bit of personality. GMB Twitter Feed, 28th September. https://twitter. com/GMB/status/1310465796422995968

Gove, M. 2001. I would happily be vice-chairman of the BBC – and then privatise it. The Times, 2nd October.

Johnson, B. 2010. So journalists at the BBC went on strike? That's news to me. Daily Telegraph, 8th November.

Johnson, B. 2012. The statist, defeatist and biased BBC is on the wrong wavelength. Daily Telegraph, 14 theMay.

Leapman, M. 1986. The Last Days of the Beeb. Coronet Books.

Loder, C. 2020. Changes Needed at the BBC. Letter to Tim Davie. 29th August. https://www. chrisloder. co. uk/sites/www. chrisloder. co. uk/files/2020-09/Tim%20Davie%2C%20Director%20General%2C%20BBC%20-%20290820. pdf

Marr, A. 2004. My Trade. Macmillan.

NFF, 2004. The Tories must fight a Culture War. New Frontiers Foundation, 6th October. https://web. archive. org/web/20071013220911/http://www. new-frontiers. org/newsarchives/displayblog. aspx?b=130

OFCOM, 2020. Media Nations 2020. 7th August. https://www. ofcom. org. uk/research-and-data/tv-radio-and-on-demand/media-nations-reports/media-nations-2020

Ponsford, D. 2020. News Uk launches Times Radio with 'Boris Johnson's 'first sit-down broadcast interview since lockdown'. Press Gazette, 29th June. https://www. pressgazette. co. uk/times-radio-launched/

Chapter 7

Making the Process the Enemy of the People: what happens when No 10 Leaks

Professor Jean Seaton has studied the history of the BBC for decades. She finds the leaks about a new Chair mark a new and disturbing precedent.

As a young, awed woman I once interviewed Hugh Carleton Greene – the man who had made fun of Himmler, who warned the *Daily Telegraph* in 1934 this was the last chance to stop Hitler, who with the young Claire Hollingsworth was last journalist out of Berlin in 1939, and whose coded and fascinating letters to his august 'Mumma' from Berlin I read in an archive last year. Greene had run the enormously successful BBC propaganda broadcasting into Germany throughout the war (with Richard Crossman). This was based on largely telling Germans, who were shot if they were found owning radios that could tune into the UK, news that they needed. He saw off an attempt to make it nothing but 'black propaganda' because, pragmatically, it would not be as effective. Of course, the object was to change minds and undermine the will to fight, but he believed you should do 'propaganda' that worked not propaganda that made you feel smug.

Later of course he was to become an innovative, brilliant BBC Director General. I was asking him about the Holocaust and he said frankly – one of his great qualities was a tremendous openness – that although he had been debriefing people from Germany about it throughout the war and had thought he understood the worst Germany could do - it wasn't until he was taken to Belsen in 1945 that he comprehended the vast enormity of it. The sight of crocodiles of neatly dressed German schoolchildren walking calmly past cattle trucks rammed with the bodies of dead Jews rocked him. I asked him what we might have learnt from the rise of Fascism? (it was 1984, so it all seemed rather remote). His answer was: that you must never let ideologues exploit democratic opportunities; that racism could never part of the speech that you admitted into the ring; that you had to see what you saw in front of you; and that you had to be wilier and recognise the scale of threat.

Greene was forced to resign after a series of rows that followed the aggressive imposition of a new Chair, Lord Hill, by Harold Wilson (though it might at this point be worth recalling that Hill was a Conservative). Hill, told by Wilson to 'sort out the BBC' came from the BBC's arch rival ITV. Sir Robert Lusty, the acting Chairman said it was like 'inviting Rommel to command the Eighth Army on the eve of Alamein. ' But Greene went.

So, who the BBC gets as a Chairman has always mattered. BBC is not a state broadcaster. Trust in the integrity of its output depends on it being seen as completely independent from Government or politicians. Consequently, its content is regulated, not by politicians, but by *Ofcom*. It is this regulation despite the collapse of the commercial broadcasters that has made *Sky* a great news channel. But what can be done about the new architecture of public life, where it is taken for granted that the current vacant public roles in broadcasting – Chair of the BBC, head of *Ofcom* – will need to be filled by people who are not merely Conservative but only from that narrow fraction that are sympathetic to the particular strand of Conservatism now in power, or members of the court around PM Johnson. After a decade of power this narrows the pool of talent to a microscopic puddle.

Appointment by leak?

The Sunday Times 'leaks' from No 10 on September 27th about the anointing of Lord Moore and Paul Dacre to the chairs of the BBC and *Ofcom* may have been intended to distract the British public from the government's performance over Covid. Getting people into a lather about the BBC is a good wheeze (because the entire British public uses it). But even if it was a Lee Cain/Cummings distraction made to see how fussed the Opposition might get it is has already done its dangerous work.

Quite independently of whether either candidate is suitable or able, the Government have politicised the process of appointing Chairs. By having a publicity pre-emptive hit, they make it peculiarly hard for an independent appointment process to work. Peter Riddell, who as the Public Appointments Commissioner, has to approve that the final outcome of the process is fair and above board. No one doubts his decency, or indeed capacity: he is a public servant of great integrity: but the procedures over which he presides have in a very significant and indeed technical way been jumped. Appointing a BBC Chair is a formally complex journey full of checks and balances. It gives the government of the day ample opportunity to influence thinking, and of course get people who are acceptable to it, but not finally determine the Chair. One of the key opportunities that the BBC has in the process is to reject candidates. This has often been a fruitful road as it forces everyone to come up with better ideas. The Civil Service has a complicated set of hurdles which are again designed to give plenty of room for argument and yet to defend the independence of the process.

The right way?

The former Conservative minister, Lord Fowler, chaired the Committee that produced the House of Lords Report on the Chairmanship of the BBC in 2007. It argued: "that the BBC is unique and we therefore believe that the appointment of the Chairman of the BBC should be subject to additional scrutiny and safeguards over and above those used for day-to-day appointments to public bodies. There should be greater separation of Ministers from the appointments process to ensure public confidence. " It went on: "There should be a duty on the Secretary of State to appoint a selection panel of at least five members including the Chairman and the independent assessor. There should be a majority of non-political members and chaired by a non-political member who is not a civil servant. "

It presciently added "we recommended that if Ministers add or subtract any names from the shortlist this should immediately be made public through a written ministerial statement to Parliament. The names and details of the candidate should not be made public but the fact of Ministerial involvement should be. " So that is one bit of the process already wrecked by this leak. It nevertheless goes on "The name of only one candidate – the one who scored highest at interview – should be passed to Ministers – specifically to avoid the appointment of a candidate who might share their political priorities. The appointment should be vetted by Parliament. " The appointment of a Chair to *Ofcom* is similarly supposed to be open and transparent.

But the really significant horse trading between the BBC and Department of Culture Media and Sport and No 10 happens **long before** the formal process opens – you do not want to end up in public complaining about a candidate who then the Government might push on through. So, t*he Sunday Times* leaks, the crowning and the drinks, compromise everything as they were meant to, turn everything into a political battle ground; compromise any of the Prime Minister's candidates, and potentially open up any other candidates to contest and opposition.

It is another classic manouvre: it is a make any opponent an enemy of the people and then destroy them tactic. Worse than that *the process becomes the enemy of the people.*

Bring on the 'candidates'/the chosen?

What of those anointed? A case could certainly be made for Moore. His biography of Margaret Thatcher is a huge achievement (compassionate and yet tough on her personally – but ferocious in the last volume about anyone who opposed her) he has been a newspaper editor, and was quite right on *Question Time to* ask about the balance of a programme that has in any case lost its way and become a nasty exercise in bear baiting. But as a climate change denier and a convicted BBC licence fee refuser how could he opine about programmes? Has he watched the summer's great drama hit *The Salisbury Poisonings,* or the deft adaption by Andrew Davies of Vikram Seth's wonderful and capacious *A Suitable Boy?* Has he listened to the new Wigmore Hall concerts or the Beethoven series or the wonderful *More or less?* on *Radio Four?* It is unlikely that he has every indulged in *Radios 1,2,5 or Radio 6* – let alone the raucous decent vulgarity of *Strictly.* Nevertheless, he would be responsible for them.

The BBC is a piece of UK soft power that is admired internationally. It is, many say, the *only* western media with the clout and reach to take on the vast new competitors trying to re-shape world thinking. Yet Moore, a clever man, has little practical international experience. A senior security official recalls a meeting about the UK and the '5 Eyes' security partners when Moore seemed to think we ought to break our relationship to French security (one of our closest partners) as we had been at odds with the French since we were still battling Bonaparte.

Paul Dacre, who reportedly thinks the BBC is run by Marxists, is something else: that would be a vindictive appointment. It would certainly not move the UK media industries into the future. The two together represent a systemic change.

Why save the BBC?

The BBC is currently, by some measure, the most trusted news organisation in the UK. It has had a great Covid 19. The pandemic has made stark the importance of citizens having ready access to trustworthy information. We are being flooded with mis and dis-information at unprecedented levels that make action over Covid even harder to deliver. We have very few industries that make what the modern world needs. Yet there is a real opportunity to unleash the power of the BBC in British interests: to cast away the chintz caveats of small minded past-seekers and allow it to shake us up, not to crowd it, let it drag itself and us into the most important bit of the modern world – what happens inside people's heads.

While apparent Trojan horse Chairs have often been surprisingly good for the BBC, nevertheless the BBC falls apart when the Chair and the DG cannot work well together. Tim Davie is a tough, charming, direct man – he ought to be able to win around a chair. Yet a degrading of our institutional proprieties' damages everything and all of us. Sadly, a Chair appointed so shoddily if he has lost authority even before he or she walks in the door.

About the Contributor

Jean Seaton is the Professor of Media History at the University of Westminster. She is also the official historian of the BBC. The latest volume of that 'Pinkoes and Traitors 1974-1987' was published in 2015. Professor Seaton is also the director of the Orwell Foundation

Chapter 8

The BBC – Our National Memory Bank

Lindsay Mackie

'AND WHEREAS in view of the widespread interest which is taken by Our People in services which provide audio and visual material by means of broadcasting, the internet or the use of newer technologies, and of the great value of such services as means of disseminating information, education and entertainment, We believe it to be in the interests of Our People that there should continue to be an independent corporation and that it should provide such services, and be permitted to engage in other compatible activities, within a suitable legal framework:

At least Her Maj is still keen on the Beeb. This, the Preamble to the Royal Charter 2016, up for renewal on 31st December 2026 (though this Government cannot bear to wait that long in its mission to destroy the BBC). And it is hard to argue with any of the sentiments summarised.

But arguing about the BBC has become, if not a national, at least a media and a Westminster obsession. Easy to see why media moguls- Rothermere, Murdoch, Barclays- would want to bring down the great beast. But harder to understand the fury against the Corporation which genuinely exists among many people and is evidenced, in part, on numerous BBC hating sites on social media. (biasedBBC.org. www.defundbbc.uk)

It's a long time since anyone referred to the BBC by its old moniker, 'Auntie'. Detractors, as well as being much more numerous than in 'Auntie's' heyday of the Sixties and Seventies, are much more vicious. The kindly, familial nickname would sit uncomfortably in the age of division and fury in which we find ourselves.

The War on the BBC

There is clearly a war on the BBC. And before we- defenders of this great public institution- work out how to keep it safe for the future we need to understand something of the nature of the opposition. And both sides – good luck with that – need to have some knowledge of the BBC's history.

The second first. The history of the BBC, since its set- up (as a private company initially until its establishment by Royal Charter as the British Broadcasting Corporation in 1927) has a set of public aims and principles which, through its Royal Charter, it must strive to fulfil. To make an obvious but perfectly fair point, you will search in vain for such high mindedness at Murdoch Towers.

Here they are:

The Charter sets out our five public purposes:

1. To provide impartial news and information to help people understand and engage with the world around them

The BBC should provide duly accurate and impartial news, current affairs and factual programming to build people's understanding of all parts of the United Kingdom and of the wider world. Its content should be provided to the highest editorial standards. It should offer a range and depth of analysis and content not widely available from other United Kingdom news providers, using the highest calibre presenters and journalists, and championing freedom of expression, so that all audiences can engage fully with major local, regional, national, United Kingdom and global issues and participate in the democratic process, at all levels, as active and informed citizens.

2. To support learning for people of all ages. The BBC should help everyone learn about different subjects in ways they will find accessible, engaging, inspiring and challenging.

The BBC should provide specialist educational content to help support learning for children and teenagers across the United Kingdom. It should encourage people to explore new subjects and participate in new activities through partnerships with educational, sporting and cultural institutions.

3. To show the most creative, highest quality and distinctive output and services.

The BBC should provide high-quality output in many different genres and across a range of services and platforms which sets the standard in the United Kingdom and internationally. Its services should be distinctive from those provided elsewhere and should take creative risks, even if not all succeed, in order to develop fresh approaches and innovative content.

4. To reflect, represent and serve the diverse communities of all of the United Kingdom's nations and regions and, in doing so, support the creative economy across the United Kingdom.

The BBC should reflect the diversity of the United Kingdom both in its output and services. In doing so, the BBC should accurately and authentically represent and portray the lives of the people of the United Kingdom today, and raise awareness of the different cultures and alternative viewpoints that make up its society. It should ensure that it provides output and services that meet the needs of the United Kingdom's nations, regions and communities. The BBC should bring people together for shared experiences and help contribute to the social cohesion and wellbeing of the United Kingdom. In commissioning and delivering output the BBC should invest in the creative economies of each of the nations and contribute to their development.

5. To reflect the United Kingdom, its culture and values to the world.

The BBC should provide high-quality news coverage to international audiences, firmly based on British values of accuracy, impartiality, and fairness. Its international services should put the United Kingdom in a world context, aiding understanding of the United Kingdom as a whole, including its nations and regions where appropriate. It should ensure that it produces output and services which will be enjoyed by people in the United Kingdom and globally.

What's the BBC for?

Famously, the purposes of the BBC, laid down by John Reith when he became its first Director general in 1927,were to 'educate, inform and entertain' the people of Britain, and the world through the World Service. THE BBC was never intended to be on the 'side' of a particular group of people, nor of Government, but this did not stop it falling foul of Churchill,

Baldwin, George Orwell, the unions (in the General Strike of 1926), Bernard Ingham (Mrs Thatcher's chief press officer) right up to the Blair Government and the dreadful Dr Kelly tragedy.

So the Corporation's inability to please all the people all the time, is written into its fabric and history. It even had its own wartime experience of 'fake news' when the Government wanted the BBC to refrain from covering the disaster of the Norwegian expedition of 1940 and to generally print success stories about the Allies, regardless of the truth. Noel Newsome, then head of BBC European services, resisted and insisted, successfully, that BBC news bulletins had to be truthful. 15 million Germans listened to the BBC, risking their lives (Newsome used to scawl 'Would you risk your life for this?" on bulletin copy that fell below standard). The BBC's reputation for truthful reporting was assured.(V for Victory. David Boyle. The Real Press 2018.)

The history of the BBC is therefore founded on utterly different principles than those of its current foes. It was set up to be a public good. It was not concerned with profit. It believed in its educative powers. It struggled, and struggles, mightily with concepts of what truth is, what news is, what impartiality is. It believes in the United Kingdom (hence its titanic struggles in Scotland today). It aims for universality- to reach every part, cultural, geographical, demographic- of the UK. And the world. It is, if you like, a strange beast to be wandering in the algorithmic world of Facebook and Twitter and the rest of social media.

The new enemies

By and large, the enemies of the BBC, those baffled or bruised or incensed by it, never actually called for its destruction.

What has changed? We can posit a number of explanations. A country divided by Brexit, by the retreat of liberalism and belief in the public state, the fracturing of viewing and listening habits, the astonishing rise and potency of social media, the devolution of the kingdom. I would add the relentless grip on print media (which instigates 'stories' and topics which are then taken up elsewhere on the media landscape) of the billionaire Press, safeguarding its monetary interests by rabidly attacking progressive values.

The attacks on the BBC centre on its elitism- supposed- its Westminster/Islington location- supposed- and its left leaning bias- supposed. For supporters of the BBC these are daft charges.

61

A small example. Recently I watched the latest *Ambulance,* the Bafta Award winning documentary series on BBC1. It had every value Reith ever dreamt of, and was wholly, wholly a million miles from the libel flung at the BBC of being metro- centric.

Matthew Syed (*Sunday Times 3rd September 2020*) made the same point

'The BBC ..is not just a broadcaster. Since 1922, if not always consciously, it has acted as a counterweight to the forces that pull at the fabric of any society ,causing it to fracture, polarise or otherwise unravel. It does this not just through great programming , but also the universal access that creates shared experiences, whether they are the Olympics, wildlife documentaries, dramas, election coverage, video clips, soap operas, news programmes,(which still attract millions of viewers) or *Gavin and Stacey* on Christmas Eve. …The BBC should be wary of any change that undermines its universality , for this expresses its most basic meaning. '

The truth is that the BBC is engulfed, through no choice of its own, in a culture war. The friends and allies of the Corporation are going to have to deal with the vaguely menacing charges of elitism/wokeness/ left leaningness/ lack of patriotism which so resemble the current US cultural confrontations .The big question is how we best do this. I would suggest three ways forward.

The BBC itself must rise to its own defence with creativity, bravery and imagination. Tell the British people what richness you provide day in day out.

Parliament must be lobbied persistently to protect this great British institution. Coming up is the review into de-criminalisation of the licence fee. MPS need to be furnished with the truth about both the licence fee, and the campaign against it.

A wider campaign must concentrate on the regions, on education, on news, on universality, on music and drama, on advice and psychological support provided by the BBC, on its unifying capacity.

 The Beeb has risen to the Covid19 challenge, in education, in music, in drama, in unbiassed coverage of the Government's statements. It has attracted high levels of trust among viewers and satisfaction with its reporting. This is what the Corporation is for- a universal service which somehow expresses a nation's character and preoccupations. *Gavin and Stacey*, programmes about otters, *You and Yours*, *6 Music* are some of our traits. It is not the fault of the BBC that it is caught up in our newer national traits of fury, resentment, anguish about the future, and political division.

About the Contributor

Lindsay Mackie. Is a writer, former journalist(The Guardian) and is now a partner in the New Weather Institute, a cooperative think tank. Her interests centre on the malign powers of global corporations and how progressive national forces can confront them. A keen supporter of savethebbc and an organiser of current attempts to do so.

Who Pays the Piper and Who Plays the Tune?

Introduction

John Mair

'Follow the Money' as ever. The BBC is only as big and good as its budget of close to £5 billion annually. Much of that is outwith its control. The licence fee level is set by government. Currently it is £157. 50 per household, rising with inflation. The level is due for review in 2022, hopefully not downwards, The principle should survive until the next Charter review in 2027. Licence fee plus commercial income-from programme and format sales-is all the BBC has.

Paddy Barwise and Peter York are about to give birth to a magnum opus on the BBC later in 2020. They give us a sneak preview in which they argue that the future and best solution is a universal household levy whether the household has a television set or not.

David Elstein is a sceptic when it comes to BBC financing. He has been a critic of the status quo for two decades. Elstein started in the BBC but has spent much of his professional life in the commercial sector. His answer is a hybrid of licence fee and subscriptions.

Likewise Robin Aitken. He is a former reporter and correspondent for the BBC who has become a fierce critic from the Right . He thinks the Corporation is out of touch, biased against the popular mood and crying out for reform. He says change or lose the licence fee.

Bernard Clark is a true media entrepreneur. He invented *Watchdog* on the BBC four decades ago and has since gone on to setting up a successful independent production company and making his fortune in the technical and compliance side of world television. He thinks the BBC is the best as the sum of its parts and would be best split into them with customers micro paying for various bits,

Finally, Professor Steven Barnett, a long time super fan of the Corporation. He looks at the ways in which the legislative and appointment manoeuvrings of Boris Johnson/Dominic Cummings might cripple or de-capitate the BBC. Whichever way you 'Follow the Money' and look at funding, the storm clouds gathering over New Broadcasting House are looking darker by the day

Chapter 9

What's the Right Long-Term Funding Model for the BBC?

What are the real pros and cons of the licence fee? What are the alternatives? And what's the right long-term model? Drawing on their forthcoming book 'The War Against the BBC', Patrick Barwise and Peter York provide the answers.

Because the BBC's enemies say ever more loudly that the TV licence fee should be abolished *this minute*, the temptation for the Beeb's supporters is to defend the current funding model to the last ditch. We disagree: there are better options. The challenge is to find a calm, rational, evidence-based, politician-free process to evaluate them, rather than just picking the one promoted by the BBC's right-wing critics.

Technically, there's no urgency: under the current BBC Charter, the licence fee (although not its level) is guaranteed until 2027. So, however much its critics huff and puff, it's here to stay till then unless the Privy Council agrees to change the model in mid-Charter.

Nevertheless, linking the BBC's core funding to households' ownership of a TV set[16] is already anachronistic and becoming more so every year. The BBC should therefore *actively argue* for the government to set up a proper independent review of the alternatives, similar to the 1985-86 Peacock Committee which looked at a BBC advertising model and firmly rejected it - despite both its chairman, Alan Peacock, and the PM, Margaret Thatcher, having initially favoured it. If, on the basis of rational evidence and analysis, a *'Peacock II'* committee recommended switching to another funding model before 2027 – which we think it would - and if both the BBC and the government agreed, the Privy Council would surely agree too.

So, what are the pros and cons of the licence fee, what are the alternatives, and what's the right long-term model?

---

[16] Or, in principle, any screen that enables them to watch TV and video.

The Actual and Mythical Pros and Cons of the Licence Fee

In 2015, the House of Commons DCMS committee discussed the licence fee's pros and cons. They said its advantages were that it was simple, secure, predictable, associated in people's minds with paying for the BBC, protected its commercial and political independence, and enabled its services to be universally available. None of these is seriously contested. They said its disadvantages were that it was regressive (the same for rich and poor households), compulsory - including for TV homes that 'do not use [the BBC's] services' - 'expensive to collect' and had a 5.5 per cent evasion rate.[17]

However, only the first of these supposed disadvantages – 'regressive' – is actually valid (although, at just three pounds per household per week, it's not in the same league as, say, the 1989 poll tax[18]): like all taxes, the licence fee is, of course, compulsory - but, unlike with many much higher ones, the number of households that pay but don't benefit is, in reality, either zero or negligible;[19] and the combined collection cost (2.8 per cent of licence fee revenue in 2018-19[20]) and evasion rate (5.5 per cent) - totalling 8.3 per cent - is, as we'll show, *much* less than the equivalent income generation and customer support costs for advertising or subscriptions.

What Are the Alternatives?

The DCMS committee listed four alternatives to the licence fee: advertising, subscriptions, a revised licence fee (or another earmarked tax) and general taxation. They also briefly considered a mixed/hybrid funding

---

[17] House of Commons, DCMS Committee, session 2014-15', 'Future of the BBC: fourth report of session 2014-15', 26 February 2015, page 71. The report also listed free-riding by some online-only homes (the 'iPlayer loophole') as another disadvantage. This loophole was closed, at least in principle, in the current Charter.

[18] Or, say, SkySports.

[19] No one knows how many of these households there are, but the number is certainly tiny. The last time household consumption of the BBC's services was measured, in 2015, it was found that 99 per cent of households consumed at least some BBC content *in a single week*. (BBC, *BBC's response to DCMS green paper: BBC charter review*, Audience appendix, 2015, http://downloads.bbc.co.uk/aboutthebbc/insidethebbc/reports/pdf/bbc_charter_review_audiences_appendix.pdf). The idea that a significant number of households are forced to pay the licence fee but consume no BBC services *over a whole year* is a myth.

[20] £103m out of £3,690 m total LF income: BBC Annual Report and Accounts 2018-19, pages 61, 208.

model but, rightly, rejected it: each funding method involves significant fixed costs, greatly reducing the efficiency of combining them.

Advertising is a non-starter. Peacock's two reasons for rejecting it in 1986 - that it would damage other advertising-funded media and distort the BBC's incentives – apply even more today, with most commercial media under serious financial pressure and the BBC facing more competition than ever. Two further reasons – not even considered by Peacock[21] – are, first, that (other things being equal) audiences demonstrably prefer not to have their viewing and listening interrupted by commercials; and, secondly, the substantial hidden overhead costs of broadcast advertising:[22] we estimate these as at least 20 per cent of advertisers' total campaign expenditure – more than double the 8.3 per cent figure for the combined collection and evasion costs of the licence fee.

Politically, the most widely touted alternative to the licence fee is a *subscription* model, although those doing the touting have – for over thirty years - been remarkably shy about revealing any specific proposals and their likely outcomes. If – and it's a big if – the government sets up a genuinely independent *'Peacock II'* review, perhaps our curiosity will finally be satisfied. At that point, we think the idea of subscriptions will, like the advertising option, come crashing to the ground. For starters, a subscription model would require every device used to access BBC TV (or any BBC service?) to have conditional access technology, so that those who had not paid could be excluded. It's unclear how long it would take, and how much it would cost, to achieve this. A subscription model would also give the BBC a financial incentive to prioritise the needs of those better able to pay - to 'segment and focus' like commercial broadcasters. And, crucially, it would no longer be a universal public service, shared by all - the core of the BBC's promise to the nation for nearly a hundred years.

To maintain the same level of content investment – the highest in the UK by far and overwhelmingly by and for Brits - the average subscription price (however structured[23]) would also need to be **much** higher than the licence fee. There are two reasons. First, because not everyone would subscribe,

---

[21] The Peacock Committee sat for over a year and its report runs to 223 pages. Yet, amazingly, it appears not to have considered these additional factors.

[22] Creative agency fees, media agency fees and commercial production costs plus the internal direct and support costs of the broadcaster's commercial airtime sales operation.

[23] There are lots of options. The main ones are (i) a single monthly fee for all BBC services and (ii) a tiered system with a lower-priced basic package and one or more higher-priced premium packages. None of this changes the fundamental problems highlighted here.

those who did so would each need to pay more to generate the same revenue. Secondly, less of this revenue would be available to invest in programmes because, like advertising, subscriptions involve much higher overhead costs[24] than the licence fee. Ask *Sky*. Even worse, these two factors would create a vicious circle: because less of the revenue would go into programmes, more households would choose not to subscribe, further reducing the revenue, and so on.

No one knows what the eventual outcome would be, and those proposing a subscription model certainly haven't said - or even published some hypothetical scenarios. But, to maintain the current level of total - and original UK - content investment, it's hard to see anything less than a 50 per cent increase in the average cost of the BBC's services for those choosing to subscribe. If those proposing subscriptions have some better projections than ours, now's the time to reveal them – show us we're wrong!

General taxation is attractive in theory, but other countries have found it even harder than other funding methods to keep politician-proof. The DCMS committee therefore rejected it, concluding that the licence fee - perhaps with some modifications - was the 'least worst' short-term option, but the best long-term funding method would be another hypothecated tax. We agree.

So What's the Right Long-Term Funding Model?

Like the DCMS committee, we think a *universal household levy* (i.e. regardless of whether the household has a TV set or any other specific device) would be better than the licence fee: the collection and evasion costs would be even lower and the fee could be made progressive, with larger and/or better-off households paying more. One option would be to collect it separately, as in Germany[25] and, now, Ireland. The alternative would be to include it with households' council tax or electricity bills, which would automatically mean that bigger, richer households paid more.

In our view, the right long-term funding model for the BBC is one of these options, that is, a *device-independent universal household levy*. Our own preference is for a progressive version, such as a small percentage supplement to council tax or electricity bills. It's worth some really clever

---

[24] Marketing, installation, billing and customer support.
[25] The German system is a universal flat fee (Euros 17.50/month - about 19 per cent higher than the UK licence fee) paid by every household, company and public institution, with exemptions for second-home owners, students and some welfare recipients.

thinking to maintain the BBC's investment in content, especially original UK content, and its 'promise to the nation' to be universal, independent and impartial in an age of fragmentation and toxic hyper-disinformation. Our democracy depends on it.

This is a perfectly soluble problem – if the options are looked at in a rational, evidence-based way. How likely that is falls outside the scope of this chapter.

About the Contributors

Patrick Barwise is emeritus professor of management and marketing at London Business School and former chairman of Which?. He has published widely on management, marketing and media.

Peter York is President of the Media Society. He is a 'capitalist tool' by background, as a market researcher (like Paddy Barwise a Patron of the Market Research Society) and management consultant. In parallel he is a social commentator, journalist, occasional TV presenter and author of eleven books, ranging from the best-selling *Official Sloane Ranger Handbook* to *Authenticity is a Con*, an attack on the cult of authenticity.

The authors' *The War Against the BBC: How an Unprecedented Combination of Hostile Forces Is Destroying Britain's Greatest Cultural Institution...And Why You Should Care* will be published by Penguin Books on 26th November 2020.

Chapter 10

New Ways of Funding the BBC?

David Elstein, former Head of Programming at Sky and Thames TV, has long argued for the BBC to adopt subscription funding. But what does that mean?

Shortly before retiring as Director-General of the BBC in September 2020, Tony Hall told Radio Four's *The Media Show* that he hoped "there will be a big debate about the best way to fund the BBC; and we should learn from other countries – are there fairer ways to pay?"

Fairness, of course, is not the only issue that swirls around the future of the licence fee; and there is not just one kind of "fairness". Hall was referring to the perceived "unfairness" to the poor of using a flat-rate fee to fund the BBC, whereby millionaires with half a dozen TV sets pay the same as pensioners and impoverished single parents.

But is it fair to other media companies, as the chair of the Commons Media Committee, Julian Knight MP, asked in September, for them to face a rival with a large guaranteed income, deployed at will to deliver entertainment rather than public service content; a rival which can compete fiercely for audiences; which can promote its radio stations on its television channels; and which can invest hundreds of millions of pounds in free online content when newspapers need digital income to replace their collapsing circulation and advertising revenues?

And then there is the fairness to society as a whole: is it fair to threaten people with criminal sanctions for failing to pay for output which in many ways is very similar to that which is readily available, either on advertiser-funded channels or subscription services?

Is it fair to provide no choice?

But is subscription a practical alternative to the licence fee?

Tony Hall's replacement, Tim Davie, in his first speech to his 19,000 public service employees, chose to refer to subscription as a direct alternative to the licence – and like his chairman, Sir David Clementi, noted that the BBC might well thrive as a subscriber service, but would inevitably shed a proportion of its audience, even if the monthly cost was no greater than the licence fee's £13: so losing its claim to universality.

They also argue that a straight switch to subscription would be "unfair" to millions of households dependent on the *Freeview* system, whose TV sets (thanks to historic BBC obstructionism) lack the conditional access modules allowing easy uptake of encrypted channels. That an upgrade is relatively cheap, and will in due course be rendered irrelevant by broadband roll-out, does not wholly remove the force of this objection.

Full conversion of BBC TV to subscription has few proponents. The most widely held view on the subscription side of the argument is that BBC public service broadcasting (PSB) content should continue to be freely available, unencrypted, with only the entertainment elements of BBC TV being offered as a subscription option.

That, for instance, was the view from another departing BBC executive, Sarah Sands, as she handed over the *Today* programme in September, and it was echoed by the formidable Dame Patricia Hodgson – former Director of Policy at the BBC and Chair of Ofcom – in an interview for Radio Four's *The World This Weekend* recently.

Such an approach dates back to at least the Peacock Report of 1986, which recommended that, in due course, BBC PSB output be financed by a Public Service Broadcasting Commission, and the remainder of its output be funded commercially; multiple reports since then have argued along similar lines.

The PSBC would also support public service content on other channels and platforms: an increasingly important objective at a time when long-term competitive pressures have squeezed PSB output from ITV and Channel 4.

What would be "fair"?

The BBC has publicly mused over replacing the licence fee with a surcharge on council tax or income tax: Hall, for one, arguing that moving away from a flat fee would be fairer to the poor. Council tax, for instance, costs the average Band H household three times the Band A level. Income tax is even more steeply progressive.

But if the BBC wants the same level of income as the licence fee affords, it would require an 11% surcharge on council tax, costing Band H homes more than double the licence fee. And replacing the licence with an income tax surcharge would result in nearly half of all households paying little or nothing for the BBC, most likely provoking cries of "unfair" from the other half. That is why split funding is so important.

The best way of defusing these potential dangers is to divide the BBC's activities and funding explicitly into public service and commercial. The BBC's news, current affairs, documentaries, arts, religion, children's, music and regional output in television, along with nearly all its radio services other than Radios 1 and 2, would fall in the first category. The second category would cover entertainment, features, drama, comedy and most of travel and nature programmes: roughly 90% of what is broadcast by BBC One, and about half of that shown by BBC Two.

If the level of public funding were half the amount raised by the licence fee, that would be sufficient to finance all the BBC's public service offerings on TV and radio, and create a much larger contestable fund for non-BBC providers than the current minuscule £20 million a year that was set aside in the last Charter review.

All kinds of "fairer" ways of funding public service content could be devised that – at this level of proceeds – ensured that no-one paid more than previously, whilst most homes would pay less: the over-75s concession of free licences could easily be re-instated. "Fairness" would prevail.

Of course, many households would choose to pay voluntarily for access to the BBC entertainment package: but there is no compulsion involved. Millions of homes pay up to £100 a month for packages from Sky and Virgin Media: that is their choice.

Enders Analysis has estimated that up to 50% of homes might choose to pay for a premium BBC service, suggesting that some £1.7 billion a year might thereby be generated. Given that this model presumed a single channel, rather than what is more likely – a suite of channels (for example *BBC Drama, BBC Comedy, BBC Arts, BBC Sport, BBC Nature*) – such a target might turn out to be too modest. And then there is the world market to address: where *Netflix* finds more than half its subscribers.

But what of universality and Freeview?

Universality is actually a very recent doctrine. BBC radio and television services took decades before they became universally available. When BBC Two was launched, at the same time as colour television, the higher fee for a colour licence became in effect a fee for receiving BBC Two.

When the Davies Report in 1999 recommended an additional digital licence fee to fund new digital BBC services, part of the reasoning was that these services would not be universally available, so should only be paid for by those choosing to receive them. The same will be true of any future BBC subscription package.

As for *Freeview*, all the BBC's public service TV content would continue to be available on that platform until such time as the system were phased out. Access to new entertainment content would require a broadband, cable or satellite connection, but it is likely that repeats would be sub-licensed to the publicly-funded channels (on terms that would need to be approved by the PSBC).

Similarly, if a BBC subscription service included a premium sports channel, highlights could be assigned to a public service channel. The main *i-Player* service would be reserved for subscribers, but PSBC funding could be used to create a version that would be free-to-air.

Of course, there can be lots of arguments about "borderline" material – is *"Planet Earth"* public service, or commercial, or both? It happens to be a highly commercial production (as are most high-end nature series) which also serves a public purpose. One way of dealing with such genres is to assign first transmission to a commercially-funded broadcaster, but for the PSBC to fund the purchase of a public service "window" for subsequent free-to-air transmission.

An obvious way of managing the split would apply to the *Proms*. The BBC *Premium* package, if it included an ambitious arts offering, might schedule the entire season live, whilst cutting a deal with the public service channel to show some concerts live and others "as live" or in excerpts (the current practice). That way, viewers as a whole are far better served, while the free-to-air public service audience loses nothing.

However, the kind of split floated by Julian Knight – whereby just the *iPlayer* service converts to subscription, leaving the current BBC channel line-up unchanged – is highly unlikely to generate enough revenue to justify the exercise.

A dynamic future BBC?

Only with a clear split between commercial and public service output can a dynamic entity be created that will invigorate the production sector and be able to compete internationally, whilst still leaving a large volume of public service content freely available, funded by a mechanism designed to revive public service output more widely.

About £1.5 billion is a reasonable estimate of what the BBC spends on public service content on radio and TV, including World Service radio. According to Ofcom, the BBC spends barely £1 billion on the direct costs of all its first run origination (including PSB), so even allowing for a healthy overhead margin, the £1.7 billion projected by Enders Analysis for subscription income would be more than enough to fund commercial output, on an increasingly large scale.

So what kind of BBC should emerge from any forthcoming negotiation with government? Tim Davie is ideally suited to managing a transition: has been running BBC Studios for six years, overseeing a large production company making content for the BBC and the commercial sector, closely linked to a distribution company that is the UK's largest, representing independent producers as well as his own in-house ones.

He is also responsible for the BBC's overseas ventures – channels and streaming services funded by a mixture of subscription and advertising – as well as one of the biggest channel packages in the UK, constituting *UKTV*'s dozen or so brands, which the BBC now both owns and operates.

This business is already capable of generating over £100 million annually from carriage fees and advertising. Running it is a channel management team that would love to incorporate a suite of BBC channels – *Drama, Sport, Comedy, Documentaries, Arts, Children's, Entertainment, Features* – into its portfolio, to match the constantly expanding *Sky* offer.

Perhaps the likeliest route to market would be to offer consumers a rich menu of options (pick three services from eight, plus UKTV, for £12 a month, say), either directly through their broadband connection, or through wholesalers like Virgin Media and Sky.

The BBC has almost from its inception – with the launch of the *Radio Times* – been engaged in commercial activity, and for the most part this should be applauded. Its commercial activities currently generate one third of its gross revenues.

The politics of transition

The BBC needs to think through the politics of any prospective change. Might ministers underwrite the BBC pension scheme deficit for a number of years as an incentive for the BBC to re-structure itself? Given the "win" that Boris Johnson would try to claim in, not just decriminalising evasion, but eliminating the licence fee as such and halving the cost to UK households of funding public service broadcasting, he should be in a generous mood.

Indeed, in due course, the subscription channels will be contributing hundreds of millions of pounds a year to the Treasury in VAT.

The BBC has shifted many of its old functions, such as transmitters, studios, outside broadcasts, graphics and – most recently – all of TV production to external or ring-fenced delivery. Devolving entertainment programming, and persuading the public to pay for it voluntarily, as recommended by Peacock 35 years ago, would be the biggest challenge yet; but there is no reason to believe that Tim Davie cannot deliver it.

About the Contributor

David Elstein is the former Head of Programming for both Thames and Sky Television. He founded one of the first independents-Brook Productions and was the founding CEO of Channel Five.

Chapter 11

BBC 2030 – Not the Last Night

**Is subscription the red line not to be crossed by the Corporation?
Bernard Clark-who invented 'Watchdog'-is a critical friend. He says
'hold your nose do it Auntie!'**

In 1983, as an Executive Producer in the BBC's Music & Arts Department,
I was invited to attend monthly meetings of senior executives to discuss a
vital question. The BBC's future.

These meetings were held on the sixth (top management)floor of
Television Centre, and presided over by then Managing Director of BBC
TV, Aubrey Singer. We were encouraged to think 'revolutionary thoughts',
before the phrase 'outside the box' had been invented, and I remember the
fateful evening I questioned whether the Licence Fee had outlived its
purpose. 'The BBC might be far better funded, and freer, if we could move
to subscription', I suggested.

"I'm afraid that is not a subject to be discussed," Aubrey said. "Off limits,"
added Brian Wenham, then Director BBC Programmes for the BBC.

I think it was Tom Gutteridge,a fellow executive producer, who then piped
up – "Why? Isn't that exactly what we *should* be discussing. If it will mean
a higher, more secure income, and less political interference, we should at
least give it serious thought."

That was the last meeting of executives that Tom and I were invited to.
Within a year, we both left the BBC, setting up separate, very successful,
independent production companies. Perhaps more tragically, Aubrey was
also gone – covertly forced out by Home Secretary Douglas Hurd, as a
precursor to the sacking of DG Alistair Milne, ultimately at the behest of
Mrs Thatcher, with the connivance of Rupert Murdoch. So much for an
independent BBC!

Radical Tories hate 'BBC Culture', perhaps because it felt like the Civil
Service, but was far more successful, and was loved and respected by the
people of Britain much more than the Conservative Government. Déjà vu?

There is an alternative...

The point then, and the point now, is that subscription is the ideal way to fund a truly independent and creative public service communication organisation, whether TV, Streaming, Internet, Radio or whatever.

We only have to look at *Netflix* to see what a part of the BBC could have become; the BBC had the content and technology years before *Netflix*, *BBC Radio* is admired, valued and consumed globally; the *BBC's Websites* are among the most visited of all. They could commercially be worth £100billion+ - without a single advert being shown. But all this is constrained by a funding model that may have been modern in 1923 but has not been good for the BBC since, yes, 1983.

I write this, not as a critic of the BBC, or indeed the licence fee, but as one of its most loving friends.

In its time, the mandatory BBC licence was a brilliant mechanism, and continued to confound sceptics, including myself, for a couple of decades after it should have been pensioned off; because everyone HAD to pay, each household got a terrific broadcaster cheaply. And because the BBC supported it, we all supported it, even though the commercial case was poor, and the editorial case even worse.

Having dragged its feet for forty years, the BBC still continues to let outsiders decide the fate of its finances. It's as if *Sky* or *Netflix* or the *Daily Telegraph* allowed the government to set its prices.

Who pulls Auntie's strings

Being commercially literate, the new DG, Tim Davie, will fully understand this; but precisely because of his experience of industry, he may not appreciate who really has been pulling the BBC's financial, and therefore editorial, strings.

In fact, it's a strange, informal alliance of usually opposing forces - the Civil Service the Establishment, and market-oriented, competing media companies like *News UK*. In their own very different ways, they have used the licence fee as a convenient strait jacket, to control or undermine the greatest communication institution in the history of the world-the BBC. That's the past, or should be: What of the future?

War footing for the BBC?

The best position for the BBC to take now is to accept that its only friends are its consumers, the people. Government, in all its guises, and of course all competitors, are the enemy, and as the BBC struggles to secure its own finances directly with the public, it will be war.

The BBC's war-room model should be similar to the positions the fledgling IT companies took in the 1990s against fearsome mega-corporate opposition, with a tight-core executive team sworn to absolute secrecy, to follow their leader come-what-may, and a bevy of fiercely focused lawyers. Ironically, it's the kind of model those who want to destroy the BBC fear most, because it's the model they use.

Tim Davie should despatch the many layers of worn-out BBC lifers, as Dominic Cummings is attempting within Downing Street/the Civil Service , and reduce it to a 'war cabinet'. Perhaps just three or four of the very best young executives he can recruit - from business and hedge-fund-ville, not academia or government. Ideally, they will regard Government and Governance with absolute suspicion and already have enough money to do it for 'BBC and Country'.

Transiting to the future.

Let's call this, 'The Transition Team', with a single purpose; to amass £3-4billion annually through subscription, without taking a single advertisement.

Do I hear the phrase – 'that's not the British way'? Correct, it's not. And it's a shame the BBC will have to use the tactics of the jungle. But if we don't want our beloved BBC to be despatched by Downing Street knaves, or owned by a FAANG (that's Facebook, Amazon, Apple, Netflix and Google), then we'd better wise up to the 2020s Battle of Britain that's coming.

While I've never seen the genial Tim Davie as a Churchill figure, we can hope that cometh the hour, cometh the person – a leader with a strong vision and even stronger persuasive arts, to grab absolute control of the BBC's finances, on behalf of its true owners – the British people.

So far Davie appears to be doing the right things. Touring the regions, being seen and heard, appointing a single Creative Director and letting her get on with the job (allegedly), and *denying* subscription in favour of the licence fee. Yes, you read that correctly. Say "absolutely no" to subscription. Because the minute that the Government or UK Corp thinks the BBC *wants* subscription, it will be banished to Room 101, or in Civil Service speak – 'shelved'.

Wapping revisited?

Securing subscription has to be a commando raid rather than a sign-posted barrage, fundamentally unlike the usual BBC way, of endless consulting and craven meetings; but Davie needs to think like an adolescent FAANG, and go for it, rather than court government approval.

The Transition Team will have only two objectives. To fight for a Public Corporation that really is owned by the public, not Government: And to secure a subscription mechanism, which allows the BBC to set its own prices. Prices, not just one price.

A multi-layered, monthly charged, bank/phone/credit card, micro payment system. Easy-to-join (not so easy to leave), tracked, with micro-payments - that Jeff Bezos will wish he invented (he sort-of has). Let's call it *BBC Subs*.

- *'Basic BBC'* - a cheap subscription for the majority who just want *BBC1, Radio, BBC Website*, with a few trimmings.
- *BBC Premium* for special events – say, 20p for a high-end arts programme, a drama series for 50p.
- *BBC Enticements* for deeper coverage of areas like news, foreign reporting, financial analysis, and niche sport.
- *BBC Worldview* - a pound or two per month for a window on the world (especially aimed at international audiences).
- *BBC Youth* – free.*

BBC Subs will be a combination of monthly subscription, and pay-per-view - more advanced than the systems that *Apple TV, Sky, Amazon* and *NOW TV* have been using to rake in billions. There are similar buttons on *Netflix*, and though the BBC doesn't advertise this, they are already wired into the BBC *iPlayer*. (Tim Davie recently confirmed that the BBC now has extensive details of 40-million *iPlayer* users)

*And let's not worry about the oldies or over-75's not being digitally savvy, most have *Facebook* and credit cards. It's the 'youngies' the BBC have to worry about, who hardly know what the BBC is. Let's give it all to them as an introductory offer for free, until they're hooked.

Making it happen. Lessons from America.

Presuming the next BBC Charter discussions complete on time by 2027, and there's a three-year transitional agreement, a conditional access viewing arrangement (what the lawyers might call this), could easily be done and dusted by 2030, when the licence fee would be junked.

Technically, this is a stroll in the park; the problems are political, cultural and 'little Englander' attitudes. That the licence fee seems more legitimate, seemly, more proper - that with subscription and VOD the BBC would be like all the other content providers – a *commercial* company. I don't believe that.

With the right leadership, the all-important 'spirit of the BBC' will thrive.

There is a model for how part of this can be achieved, ironically at the hands of one the BBC's more successful Director Generals. Take a bow Mark Thompson, béte noire of Murdochville and amoral operators like George Osborne. Thompson has done for the *New York Times* what the BBC now needs.

Bypassing news vendors, subsidies, FAANGS, or selling out its soul, the *New York Times* has been financially transformed from an increasingly impoverished print newspaper, dependent on cover sales, into a vibrant, multi-platform phenomenon - almost entirely through subscription. In August 2020 they reported 6.5 Million subscribers. Their digital revenue is more than that for print. They have now been able to hire an additional five hundred journalists, with more to come, the kind of virtuous circle entirely available to the BBC. Thompson's basic tenet, and a lesson to us all – in a swirling, Trumpian, media world out there-is that more than enough people really will pay for truly independent quality.

Mark Thompson had the confidence to back that simple faith, the skill to make it work and the courage to give it a try. Tim Davie should definitely take him out to lunch.

Take courage, Tim.

As Britain and the world enter the twilight of terrestrial television, as newspapers have faced their own Dunkirks, Davie and his team need to find that same confidence in reinvention. The upside is a pot of gold at the end of the BBC rainbow, but failure to act decisively could lead to a much-diminished national broadcaster in terminal decline.

The year after next, the BBC celebrates its 100th Anniversary. There will be much '*Ruling of Britannia*', much '*Landing of Hope and Glory*', but the less melodic counterpoint is that it's also a hundred years of being served by government-controlled funding. Obviously not slavery, but not freedom, either.

For better or worse, the *Last Night of the Proms* is about the past, as is the licence fee, but the past not an option for any media company. Or else the 100th Anniversary might become the *Last Night of the BBC*.

About the Contributor

Having joined the BBC as a cost clerk, Bernard Clark went on to be a BBC Correspondent, originate *Watchdog*, before becoming an Independent Producer. His Company, Lion Media (Singapore), now runs many streaming services across Asia, Australia, Japan and Europe. His book, *a Mother Like Alex*, became a best seller for Harper Collins

Chapter 12

Why We Need to Talk about the Licence Fee

The BBC's licence fee is a unique privilege which has underpinned its growth and guaranteed its universality. But the licence fee is not a right; it has to be earned says Robin Aitken.

With all the comment engendered by the reform programme of the BBC's new Director-General, Tim Davie, it might seem prosaic to focus on the question of the annual licence fee. But preserving the licence fee (or an equivalent like a 'household charge') is *the* central ambition of the Corporation's top management. Davie's reformist agenda can only be understood in the context of the campaign, now underway, to persuade a sceptical government to extend the unique privilege that the licence-fee represents.

The licence fee, in existence now for nearly 100 years, has proved to be the foundation on which the whole institution rests. Its introduction, in 1923, allowed the fledgling broadcaster to establish itself, to thrive and finally to become the pre-eminent cultural force in British society. However sustained complaints about the BBC's lack of impartiality, particularly over Brexit, have focused attention on how the BBC is funded. The Corporation's opponents know that revoking the licence-fee privilege and forcing the Corporation to become a subscription service would irreversibly weaken its influence.

The reforms being suggested by the new D-G are designed to propitiate critics and thereby protect the licence-fee.

A little light history

The -fee's origins were grounded in the realities of broadcasting at the beginning of the 20th century. Early radio technology could only exploit part of the wireless spectrum; inevitably there was cross-border competition for the available wavelengths. As governments around the world woke up to the potential of radio it was clear that the allocation of wavelengths would involve international treaties. This was to ensure that radio stations in adjacent countries – France and Germany say - would not broadcast on the same wavelength.

There was a series of international conventions which allocated wavelengths and which led to the establishment of the 'Radio Regulations' - still in operation today. Because of the shortage of spectrum, radio was ,in its early days, a 'natural monopoly' in many countries including Britain and this raised an immediate problem; how to ensure fairness to all sides?

Politicians had quickly come to understand that radio presented a new and powerful way of connecting with citizens but were aware of the dangers inherent in monopoly broadcasting: the ever-present potential for misuse by unscrupulous authority. Radio has often been harnessed by dictators for the purposes of propaganda which is why the BBC's first Royal Charter in 1927 came to lay the duty of 'impartiality' on the newly created British Broadcasting Corporation. Even when the BBC was still a private company John Reith could write, in 1924:

"The company operates as a public utility service and it is of great importance that this should be definitely recognised" (i)

Reith was here adumbrating the notion of 'public service broadcasting' but this idea – of a service for all – was always more popular on the Left than the Right. The American scholar, Lincoln Gordon, writing in 1938 about the emergence of 'public corporations' in Britain (of which the BBC was the prime example) wrote as follows:

"Its greatest appeal , naturally, has been to leaders of socialist thought and of the Labour Party who have seen in it a technique for the successive nationalisation of all basic industries in the course of a gradual transition to a socialised economy" (ii)

So from its earliest days the BBC's natural allies were on the Left while it was an object of some suspicion on the Right. The BBC understood that only by sticking to the principle of impartiality could it protect the licence-fee.

New World, Old Money

Try this counter-factual exercise. Imagine that the BBC's position as the monopoly broadcaster remained intact, that it had always faithfully fulfilled its obligations to impartiality, and was the only source of British-originated radio and television programmes available . In such a world the case for a licence fee would be unanswerable; every person would use the service so everyone must pay. But the real world is not like this at all ; we have a multiplicity of sources available to us at the touch of a keyboard. The era of monopoly broadcasting is a bygone era – but the monopoly funding mechanism is still with us. Which means the BBC has had to develop new arguments to justify its privilege.

The BBC has turned to a broader argument to defend its position; it now rested its case for the licence-fee on the desirability of the service it provided. The BBC said, in effect, 'we are a public good and therefore we deserve our hypothecated tax revenue' and for many decades now that is the argument that has prevailed. Governments, of all political stripes, have obliged the BBC by supporting the tax; in every renewal of the BBC's Royal Charter (the next due in 2027) The fee has been maintained, embedded in legislation. But that consensus is now under threat because too many people are questioning the underlying assumption about the 'good' the BBC says it delivers. There is a large constituency in the country, mainly, but not exclusively, on the right, which feels the BBC no longer understands them or their aspirations and no longer speaks to them or for them. There has been growing disillusion with the BBC's interpretation of 'impartiality' and a feeling that the Corporation has breached its promises.

Brexit Fallout

Partly this sharpening of the focus is down to Brexit; that issue was one where the BBC demonstrably failed in its duty of impartiality. I say 'demonstrably' advisedly. Proving that the BBC is biased is no easy thing; allegations are always open to the objection that they are merely subjective criticisms. The BBC routinely rejects charges of bias and says the fact it gets criticism from both Right and Left is proof of balance. But this argument runs counter to how many people on the right actually experience the BBC - and on the Brexit issue methodical monitoring has proved their point.

In the late 1990s Lord Pearson of Rannoch, a UKIP peer and one-time adviser to Mrs Thatcher, set out to prove that BBC programmes were biased against Eurosceptics. Working with the think-tank Global Britain he invested in a media-monitoring operation called *News-Watch (iii)* run by David Keighley , an ex-senior publicist for BBC News and Current Affairs. Starting in 1999 Keighley has gone, line by line, through thousands of hours of broadcasting and tabulated the results. During periods of intense debate about Europe the number of speakers on important programmes like *Today* or *Newsnight* who were Remain or Leave was noted and tabulated.

The amount of time each side was given was meticulously totted up and later published in clear tabulated form. What *News-Watch's* successive reports have shown is that BBC output massively favoured the Remain side over a period of decades. The *News-Watch* archive provides a sound evidential base for indicting the BBC of bias but it confines itself to a small number of issues of issues of interest to the political right : Brexit, immigration and climate-change. My further contention, based on lived experience and many years of research , is that that *all* BBC output is coloured by the BBC's core philosophy – a liberal-left 'woke' credo policed by the implementation of an *'Overton Window'* (End notes 1) which excludes (mainly right-wing) voices and viewpoints.

Where to next?

These complaints against the BBC are not new but there is a feeling that things are coming to a head after many years. The BBC has recently been complaining about cuts to its income; and though it still receives just shy of £5bn in domestic licence-fees and overseas programme sales, that income is falling. Tory governments of the past five years have not been so indulgent of an organisation they distrust. In 2015, in return for an inflation-matching increase in the licence-fee the BBC was forced to accept that from 2020 it would have to fund the concession of free TV licences for the Over-75s from its own resources – an annual sum of over £700 million.

But the licence fee is still a very valuable privilege. Essentially a tax on every person who owns a television the crucial thing about it is its predictability. The BBC has been able to plan ahead knowing, give or take, what next year's revenue will be. Every other commercial broadcaster has to satisfy the whims of public taste or go out of business; the BBC has been in the comfortable position of knowing that its future was assured. Until now that is.

The biggest problem the BBC faces is loss of trust and this has come about because in a multi-media world the BBC has become un-moored from the principles which governed it as a monopoly broadcaster. In those days, under constant, jealous scrutiny from both sides of the aisle, impartiality was a BBC fetish built into all its output; now, when the BBC is just one broadcaster among many, that core principle is perceived by many to have been abandoned. The BBC has become increasingly brazen about advertising its own political allegiances and growing numbers of the audience have noticed and have reacted. And in Boris Johnson and his chief adviser Dominic Cummings they have a government that seems quite prepared to strip the BBC of its privileges. (v)

That is why the new D-G, Tim Davie has begun to speak about reform; it is because he recognises the need to engage with the Corporation's critics to stave off irreversible changes to funding. Recent BBC Directors-General have all been big on the need for 'diversity' in the BBC's workforce. What this has come to mean in practice is that the BBC now enforces skin-colour/sexual orientation hiring quotas so that numbers match proportions in the general population. But all this does is ensure that BBC workers superficially *look* like Britain; what is needed is a true diversity that ensures the BBC *thinks* like Britain. Mr Davie has hinted that this is the direction he wishes to move in but for an organisation which has for decades been a left-liberal monoculture that will be a very difficult task. It would mean hiring more people with right-wing opinions and making BBC newsrooms welcoming places for social conservatives.

Whether that is realistic will become apparent in the coming months ; but time is short and the Corporation's enemies are circling. There is to be a formal review of the current Royal Charter in 2022; if no tangible progress has been made by then the BBC will probably forfeit the licence-fee from 2027.

About the Contributor

Robin Aitken was a BBC reporter for 25 years ending his career on The Today Programme. In 2007 his book 'Can We Trust The BBC?' (Continuum) was published, (new edition Bloomsbury 2013). In 2018 'The Noble Liar' (Biteback) was published - revised edition 2020. Over the years he has written many articles about the BBC for national newspapers and magazines. In 2014 he was awarded the MBE for his work as co-founder of The Oxford Food Bank – a food rescue charity.

References

(i) John Reith – later the BBC's first Director-General in '*Broadcast over Britain*' (Hodder and Stoughton 1924) p 57 .
(ii) Lincoln Gordon *The Public Corporation in Great Britain* Oxford University Press 1938 . p   3
(iii) Polling in 2020 has shown that while the BBC is more highly trusted than other UK media trust has dropped sharply among certain groups; a global survey of 40,000 people carried out by the Reuters Institute asking about the BBC's 'trustworthiness' found that among those who defined themselves as 'left-wing' or 'right-wing' trust in BBC news had fallen in the last two years by 20%. See Reuters Institute for the Study of Journalism , Digital News Report 2020

(iv) previously Minotaur Media Tracking see https://news-watch. co. uk/
(v) In 2004 Mr Cummings, then running a think-tank called *New Frontiers,* labelled the BBC the 'mortal enemy' of the Conservative Party in a blog that called for the undermining of the BBC's credibility and the establishment of a British *Fox News.* In March 2020 Cummings was reported to have outlined plans to 'whack the BBC' with a range of measures designed to weaken it.

End Note

(1) The *Overton Window* named after researcher Joseph P. Overton; it offers a taxonomic framework for analysing public discourse. For further discussion of this see the author's own book *'The Noble Liar; what needs to be done now?'* (Biteback 2020) pp 120- 21

Chapter 13

Johnson's Plan for the BBC: Decapitation?

Boris Johnson's Conservative government has signalled its intent to destabilise and downsize the BBC. Although its short-term options for inflicting damage are limited, recent reports that the government has chosen two committed right-wingers - with a long history of visceral opposition to the BBC – to chair the Corporation and its regulator suggest a strategy of top-down evisceration. Professor Steven Barnett,,

How does a government intent on dismantling the BBC actually go about its wholesale destruction? Even at the height of Thatcherite supremacy, this was an entirely theoretical question: while Margaret Thatcher and her acolytes genuinely believed that the BBC of the 1980s was a hotbed of far Left conspiracists intent on bringing her government to its knees, she was at least surrounded by a Cabinet of largely level-headed and talented politicians who understood the BBC's contribution to Britain's creative and democratic welfare.

The Boris Johnson government of 2020 is very different: a leader accustomed to a print journalism environment where he can lie with impunity, dominated by a chief adviser who believes the BBC to be the Conservative Party's "mortal enemy", and with little time for a broadcaster that offers him nothing but awkward interviews. Add to this a thumping electoral victory in which Tory moderates were marginalised and the Johnson faithful infuriated by a wholly confected row about BBC "bias", and the result is a perfect recipe for taking a sledgehammer to an institution for which few in his party hold much affection.

Options for radical change

How could this be done? In practice, this is not necessarily an easy proposition. There are really only three levers of direct influence available to an incoming government intent on inflicting damage: change the terms of the BBC Charter and/or the accompanying Agreement; slash its income or change its revenue model; or change its governance and/or the governing personnel. Unfortunately , the Charter was sealed two Prime

Ministers ago in 2016 and lasts until December 2027, including a commitment to the licence fee as the funding model for the same period. The current agreement on the licence fee rising with inflation lasts until mid-2022, though of course this has not prevented an early assault on BBC revenues via a serious threat to remove criminal sanctions for non-payment of the BBC licence fee. If it goes ahead, that will cost the BBC at least £200 million a year – a big hit in the current environment, but not terminal.

Bring on Lord Moore. . .

In the short term then, a government intent on destruction is left with governance: who runs the BBC and how. With immaculate timing for this government, David Clementi the current BBC Chairman's term comes to an end in April 2021. Although technically there is a formal and transparent process of finding a successor overseen by the Public Appointments Commissioner, in practice the government of the day can and does make the decision. And according to a clearly well sourced front-page story in the *Sunday Times* at the end of September 2020, the PM has effectively settled on his man for the job: (Lord) Charles Moore, a high Tory hard-line Brexiteer who previously edited the *Spectator, The Sunday* and The *Daily Telegraph*. Apart from his contempt for the EU and his passionate support for the Brexit cause, there are two further issues on which Moore's views are well documented: the BBC and climate change.

He has never concealed his visceral hostility to the BBC, his conviction that it is dominated by left-wing thinking, and his fervent belief that it needs to be reduced to a small core of elite services. In November 2019, he was quoted in the *Financial Times* as arguing that the BBC should be broken up with "certain bits" such as arts and documentary channel BBC 4 "allowed to survive" through voluntary membership modelled on the National Trust of British historic landmarks. In February 2020 , he wrote in his *Telegraph* column: "Any declining organisation needs to develop its strengths and jettison its weaknesses. " He earmarked just two services, *Radio 3* and *Radio 4*, as BBC strengths and continued: "Here are some weaknesses: entertainment channels, including *Radio 1* and *Radio 2*, which could be better done commercially; a website which crushes competition; a massive, talent-destroying bureaucracy; and, yes, bias. "[26]

Moore was fined £250 in 2008 for refusing to pay his licence fee (as well as paying an additional £550 to the BBC in costs). Rather than demonstrating any contrition, he used a column last year to speculate on

26. https://www. telegraph. co. uk/news/2020/02/18/bbc-must-saved-imperial-folly/

how anti BBC campaigners might successfully launch a mass refusal to follow his example. He wrote: "So what is the best way to refuse to pay?. . . A strike by a million fee-payers would deprive it of four per cent of its income, a severe knock.... How about bringing an action against it, refusing to pay one's licence fee until the case is settled?"[27] And this year he announced that he was "wondering whether to refuse to pay my licence all over again. I am reluctant, since last time it cost me £800, but one reads that non-payment will not be pursued while the plague lasts". [28]

In addition, Moore is a fully paid-up member of the 'climate change deniers club'. Since 2015, he has been a trustee of the *Global Warming Policy Foundation*, a charity set up by former Chancellor and fellow denialist Nigel Lawson that describes itself as "open-minded on the contested science of global warming" (a barely coded statement of scepticism about the overwhelming weight of scientific evidence) as well as being "deeply concerned" about the costs of climate policies. In April 2017, he argued for a "bonfire of green regulations", drawing attention (with apparently no hint of humour) to the unseasonal snow that arrived in October 2008 as the House of Commons passed the Climate Change Act. It was, he said, the first October snow in London for 74 years and yet "only five MPs took note of this divine portent and dared oppose the Climate Change Bill". [29] In June 2018, he praised Trump's "courage and wit to look at 'green' hysteria and say: no deal". [30]

How to manipulate governance of the BBC...

It is hard to imagine anyone more unsuited to be Chairman of the BBC, but what exactly are the Chairman's powers given that its objects and public purposes are laid down in some detail in the 2016 Royal Charter? After abolition of the BBC Trust in 2016, day-to-day governance of the BBC now rests with the Unitary Board of 14 members, whose composition is clearly delineated in the Charter: a Chair and four non-executive directors representing each of the nation states, all appointed by government; four executive members of the BBC, including the Director General; and five further non-executive members appointed by the Board after nomination by an independent Nominations Committee – headed by the BBC Chair. In

[27]. . https://www. telegraph. co. uk/politics/2019/04/07/should-us-think-bbc-biased-against-brexit-refuse-pay-license/
[28]. https://www. spectator. co. uk/article/the-benefits-of-the-coronavirus-era
[29]. https://www. telegraph. co. uk/news/2017/04/28/brexit-britain-cant-thrive-without-cheap-energy-need-bonfire/
[30] https//www. telegraph. co. uk/politics/2018/06/01/donald-trump-has-courage-wit-look-green-hysteria-say-no-deal/

theory, then, the freedom of a maverick Chair systematically to undermine the BBC may be constrained by other board members, given that the government has direct powers to appoint only 5 out of 14. [31]

In practice, however, the government potentially has considerably more leverage. First, through the Nominations Committee, it can ensure that the Board appoints more compliant and government-friendly non-executives to the Unitary Board. Second, Article 21(6) of the Charter states ominously that "The total number of members, the number of non-executive members and the number of executive members may, with the agreement of the BBC, be amended by Order in Council", a Parliamentary device over which the government has complete control[32]. In other words, should the government decide unilaterally to increase Board numbers in order to outvote those resisting Johnson's destructive impulses, the only obstacle would be the BBC itself risking a constitutional crisis by disagreeing with any expansion. It is difficult to see such a confrontation ending well for the BBC.

.... and its regulator

Under the new governance arrangements, defenders of the BBC might look to *Ofcom* to rescue the Corporation from devastation. Following abolition of the BBC Trust, it now has responsibility for ensuring that the BBC fulfils its Mission and promotes the public purposes enshrined in the Charter. It is now up to *Ofcom* to establish an Operating Framework for the BBC (in accordance with its Charter obligations) and then monitor compliance. In theory, an *Ofcom* that was wholly committed to its statutory duty to "promote the interests of citizens" could be an effective line of defence against a BBC Unitary Board intent on a radical cull of services.

Boris Johnson and Dominic Cummings appear to have thought of that, too. The same *Sunday Times* 'sources' that told Tim Shipman, its political editor, that Moore was "close to a done deal to be BBC Chairman" also claimed that Johnson had asked former *Daily Mail* editor and fellow BBC hater Paul Dacre to be the next chair of *Ofcom*, following the retirement of Lord Burns at the end of the year. Some online commentators compared this putative coup to Trump's determination to pack the US Supreme Court with Conservatives. Labour peer Adonis commented: "if true this is

---

[31] One of these, the Northern Ireland member, is yet to be appointed pending a new NI Executive.

[32]http://downloads. bbc. co.
uk/bbctrust/assets/files/pdf/about/how_we_govern/2016/charter. pdf

Cummings operating straight out of the Trump playbook with the intent to undermine our democratic institutions. "

Neither appointment is a done deal, but we can expect full-throated endorsement for this decapitation strategy from a predominantly right-wing press that has relentlessly attacked the BBC over many years for both ideological and commercial reasons. It is no coincidence that Rupert Murdoch has just launched *Times Radio* to complement his *TalkRADIO* and *TalkSPORT* stations, each designed to take on BBC radio. While *Times Radio* targets the *Radio 4* audience, *TalkSPORT* will be launching bids for exclusive rights to radio sports commentaries that have long been a mainstay of *BBC Radio5*. Both stations will, under a Dacre regime, be guaranteed a sympathetic hearing for complaints of excessive market domination by the BBC, as of course will anyone complaining about left-wing bias in news coverage.

And if the rumours are false?

It is perfectly possible that the *Sunday Times* briefing was deliberately timed to distract attention from bad Covid news, and is no more than malevolent kite flying by Cummings: another dead cat to join the moggy mortuary which he routinely populates. Conservative commentator Peter Oborne was certainly unconvinced when he tweeted: "This is feeding Dacre to the papers to distract attention from lockdown etc. Read the story carefully. Our friend 'No 10 sources' and our other friend 'Whitehall sources' loom large. Note the application process hasn't been opened for either job. Translation: load of bollocks".

But the very idea that such overtly partisan, committed right-wingers – with a long history of loathing for the organisations they will be overseeing – are being seriously considered is testament to the contempt with which Boris Johnson and his disciples are treating internationally admired British institutions. And if the story does turn out to be nothing but a calculated trolling of those who value the BBC, what does that tell us about the politicians taking us through the biggest crisis this country has faced since the war? We are not in safe hands.

About the Contributor

Steven Barnett *is* Professor of Communications at the University of Westminster and an established writer, author and commentator, who specialises in communications policy and regulation. Over the last 35 years, he has advised ministers and shadow ministers across the political spectrum, has given evidence to Parliamentary committees and has served several times as specialist adviser to the House of Lords Communications Committee. He is on the editorial and management boards of British Journalism Review, and was for many years an *Observer* columnist. Books include The Rise and Fall of Television Journalism (Bloomsbury, 2011) and Media Power and Plurality (with Judith Townend, eds, Palgrave, 2015).

How Big a BBC?

Introduction

John Mair

The BBC sees itself as a 'universal broadcaster', the critics say is it 'Imperialist' populating areas of media that have, or should have nothing to do with it. John Birt as BBC Director-General was superb at driving it into new digital spaces like online news long before the British printed press woke up and smelt the algorithms. They have been trying, and failing, to play 'catch-up' ever since. Hence the cries of 'foul'.

Wherever there is a new broadcast space, the BBC like an amoeba moves to fill it. Online-tick, iPlayer-tick, Box sets -tick, Podcasts-tick. But does that detract from its core public service broadcast purpose?

Critics think so and it seems to be a view taken aboard by the new Director General Tim Davie who spoke in his manifesto address to staff of 'no linear expansion'.

Michael Wilson has been round the broadcasting block, especially in Northern Ireland, for many years. He looks at the case for bringing *BBC Three*-a 'yoof' channel taken into cyberspace to find an audience(it failed. The internet is very crowded!)-back to terrestrial television. He finds that case 'not proven'

Liam McCarthy was at the sharp local end of the BBC in local radio. He managed three stations. Now he has converted that into an academic dissertation and a doctorate. He offers some wise advice to Tim Davie on rebuilding the BBC. He defies the current Corporation conventional wisdom and says it should be from the bottom up. The consolidation/collapse(you decide)of 'local' commercial radio stations into national networks many in essence juke boxes ,the still born nature of Jeremy Hunt's local TV experiment and the long (and not so slow) decline of the local press does not bode well for localism and local democracy. Maybe that moment in media has passed.

One thing is certain. Whether by his, or the Government's, design or accident, the BBC which Tim Davie leaves behind in five (?) years' time will be smaller and much more focussed. The Empire has reached its zenith.

Chapter 14

To Three or not to Three? That is the Question

The words 'young people' and the channel 'BBC Three' perhaps gets more mentions than any others in the BBC's Annual report for 2020. Political antennas are twitching in Broadcasting House and Auntie is responding. Is this short-term rhetoric or a real strategic pivot? Michael Wilson explores

While audiences in all age groups increased as the Covid-19 restrictions forced many of us to screens of all size to fill our leisure time, the long-term trend for the under 30s is away from the BBC. This is a key issue that concerns Ofcom, the Government (as a policy issue not just a political one) and the BBC itself.

Enders Analysis recently reported that viewing of *BBC Three* content, including *BBC Three* programmes shown on other BBC linear TV channels, is down 72 per cent since the channel went online (figures up to November 2019).

Ofcom did not mince its words in its last annual review of the BBC:

"If young people don't consider the BBC as a core part of their viewing, then it may be hard to encourage them to pay the licence fee which will have significant implications for the BBC's revenue and its ability to deliver its Mission and Public Purpose."

If the BBC doesn't have an audience then the justification for the universal licence fee begins to dramatically weaken. A vicious circle of reducing funding, reducing scale and reducing scope.

The BBC responded in May 2020 in its annual report. Its two-year plan aims to increase engagement with young people and has proposed nine action points including shifting commissioning spend, more boxsets on the *iPlayer*, investment in *BBC Sounds*, a 'story-led' approach to news plus a new news app and better tracking and research.

The action point that gained the most interest and column inches was this:

"Exploring the options available to BBC Three in developing its profile online and possibly through the restoration of a linear channel."

Is Three really the magic number?

Should the BBC be reallocating significant sums chasing just one part of the whole audience? Indeed are 'young people' just one audience – of course not, they have as varied interest, backgrounds and media consumptions habits as any other demographic, perhaps more so.

This is at the core of the BBC's problem with a young audience. It takes huge resource to get volume, it takes even bigger resource to get reach. The success of *Netflix* is that it caterers for niches and growing their business model by delivering content to underserved audiences.

Broadcasting on linear television is expensive – you need to have schedulers, engineers, transmission teams, big infrastructure networks, pay for satellite space and DTT spectrum. Many of these costs fall away – or are much smaller – in an on-demand world.

YouTube has a bigger audience, in terms of young people, than the BBC and it is not a TV channel; Netflix pulls large audiences, it is not a TV channel; *Disney+* has millions of subscriber and it is not...you get the point.

In August 2020 at the Edinburgh Television Festival Fiona Campbell, the *BBC Three* channel controller, told the audience she met with a senior *Netflix* executive in 2017 who 'said he felt like linear would be around for another decade'. Well if the BBC decided to relaunch a linear service it would take time to launch so almost half that decade could have already passed!

Besides the BBC delivers huge results with some online content. There have been close to 40m separate requests to watch the adaptation of Sally Rooney's *Normal People,* via the BBC *iPlayer,* with many binge-watching the series. However it must be pointed out that, even though the BBC claims *Normal People* as a huge hit with young people, 60 per cent of those viewing on the *iPlayer* were older than 35!

The *BBC Three* television audience was never huge. It was 22 per cent in 2015/16 when it was a linear television service. Now remember that's 22 per cent of the 16-34 audience, not the total audience. Since *BBC Three* was taken off linear television in March 2016 its weekly reach with the 16-34 demographic has levelled off at around at eight per cent.

The BBC annual report for 2020 talks about boosting funding for *BBC Three* by £40m (to around £80m) and then states that cuts have to be made in other channels and genres to accommodate that.

These cuts mean many painful headlines about BBC job losses and service reductions will outstrip any wins in the under-30s audience for months to come.

The annual plan rightly praises the strong performance of *BBC Three* scripted programming including *Fleabag, Killing Eve* and *Normal People*. As well as being available on the *iPlayer* that also have slots on *BBC One* after the *BBC News at Ten* where top *BBC Three* shows are scheduled three nights a week. Other successes have included *My Left Nut, Killed By My Debt (which won a Bafta), the Stacey Dooley documentaries* and *RuPaul's Drag Race*.

The BBC annual report states:

"Our research evidence shows that there is a big available audience on linear television and the BBC could reach them if we move decisively. So there is potentially a strong case for restoring *BBC Three* as a linear channel as well as an online destination."

Utter rubbish. The success of these *BBC Three* programmes is because they are on the main *BBC One* service. That is where they find their audience,

A confused argument

The debate around returning *BBC Three* to linear television is confused, more aimed perhaps at delivering a regulatory tick, than a new audience. As the young audience moves to on-demand then so should the BBC. The iPlayer will be the entry point for the BBC in the years ahead. Not just for young eyeballs but all viewers – so far in 2020 there has been a 60 per cent plus increase in programme requests via the *iPlayer* compared to 2019.

The BBC even admits a linear channel would be secondary in audience to online:

"While young people would continue to predominately watch *BBC Three* content online."

The additionality of a linear channels would be marginal, the costs would be significant at a time when all budgets are under review. Sure, invest in the content, but think radically about the distribution.

High-quality *BBC Three* programming can and should be shown on *BBC One*. Just like dramas such as *Line of Duty* and comedy like *Have I Got News For You* moved from *BBC Two* to *BBC One*.

This happened too when BBC Three launched in 2003 and made its name with hits like *Little Britain and Gavin* and *Stacey*. These programmes transferred to main channels. Indeed the biggest show on television for Christmas 2019 was a *Gavin and Stacey* reboot on BBC One.

That's what good programming and development means – making hits, developing (British) talent and then selling to other international broadcasters to help fund more programming and bring less reliance on the licence fee. *BBC Three's* commissioning team has been very good at finding 'hits', but it's impossible to translate across a whole channel – both on cost grounds and the shortage of stand-out ideas.

There is no reason why *BBC Three* online hits cannot move to existing linear channels and grow – *BBC Three* does not need its own channel. Indeed in her Edinburgh speech the *Three* controller also admits the decision is part of a 'bigger picture' and costs have to be managed.

The reason these hit programmes have shown 'there is a big available audience on linear television' is that not just young people are watching. The argument stands – 'hit' programming attracts large audiences across all age groups.

The BBC clearly defines a 'hit' as a programme that get a high volume of audience and/or critical acclaim. But a hit should also be a programme that serves very well a niche audience, may not get a high audience rating, but is also critically successful.

Back to that Edinburgh speech and Campbell said, "At the end of the day, we are trying to make content to get to the most amount of people."

The BBC always says it doesn't chase the ratings – but the truth is a commissioner or channel heads are judged as being good or effective on the volume of audience, not the reach of the service. Look at their channel – and often their personal – social media feeds, it's the big audiences and the awards they celebrate, not the new audiences reached.

How the BBC reacts

The 2020 BBC Annual Report also states:

"We'd be wrong not to back a service that is doing better than anyone could have ever conceived."

This is BBC-speak for we have been told to 'back a service' which is now politically important. The report beautifully contradicts itself too stating, "Investing in digital services means the BBC is better meeting the demands of audiences, particularly younger people."

So do young people want 'linear' or 'digital'? Or is the BBC just smattering the words 'young people' in the document as much as it can to show they are on the corporate radar. The shiny new corporate buzz phrase!

Interestingly in his maiden speech as DG, Tim Davie set out four new priorities to make the BBC a '21st century organisation' – one of them was to 'extract more from online' and no mention of *BBC Three* in the speech at all. Perhaps the new guard has already decided the future of *BBC Three…*

This chapter (now updated) was originally published in Michael Wilson and Neil Fowler's Bite-Size Public Affairs Book "The Generation Game: Can the BBC win over today's young audience?" Published Summer 2020

About the Contributor

Michael Wilson is an experienced chief executive, managing director, board member and editor-in-chief with more than 30 years' business and leadership experience in the content creation, broadcasting, media, communications and digital sectors. He has held senior roles *Sky News, Five News, UTV Media plc* and *ITV*.

Chapter 15

Bottom Up. Rebuilding the BBC

Dr Liam McCarthy argues that the BBC must retain its strong local journalism and recognise that BBC local radio, through its working practices, contribution to diversity and deep connections with its audience, can be a force in the re-imagining the BBC.

Local journalism is in a crisis that has been accentuated by the negative effects of Covid 19 on advertising revenue. Four fifths of ILR franchises and local newspaper titles are owned by just seven companies with shareholder value a factor in driving newsroom closures and cuts. A local democratic deficit is developing and the BBC as a public service broadcaster must safeguard its local journalism. In his first speech to staff Tim Davie recognised 'the connection that a strong local radio station builds with an audience', he now needs to build on this when executing his aim to make the BBC 'less rather than more London-based'. Diversity also featured strongly in this speech and he argued that action is a priority noting 'the gap between rhetoric and action remains too big' (Davie, 2020)(i). Since 1967 BBC local radio has a strong, if not unblemished, track record in diversity including the recruitment of staff from outside of Davie's 'BBC type'.

The new DG needs to examine four key areas in local radio that could impact on his reforms to the wider BBC; securing local journalism, making the right cuts, embracing diversity, and building deeper audience connections.

Local media; Securing BBC local radio journalism.

Given the near collapse in local commercial radio news the BBC has a responsibility to retain its own local journalism. After thirty years of light touch regulation and consolidation *Global* and *Bauer* now own four out of five of the 227 analogue local licences in England. Both are replacing local stations with national brands such as *Greatest Hits Radio, Capital* and *Smooth Radio.* Ofcom rules still require limited regional programming but locally sourced news provision is all but gone with dozens of local newsrooms closing in August 2020 alone (*The Guardian,* 2020). (ii) It is little different in local newspapers where five companies now own four out of five local titles *(MediaReform. org)*(iii). In the last 15 years over 250 local titles have closed *(Press Gazette August 2020)* and there is a continuing hollowing out of the remaining newsrooms. For example, this summer Reach PLC with 70 major local titles has cut a further 550 jobs across the country *(The Financial Times, July 2020)*(iv).

Especially at this time when local is becoming more rather than less important it is vital that the BBC retains its core local newsrooms across the country. They contribute hundreds of local stories to the pool of BBC journalism, capturing the essence of local debate. Regular listeners to BBC local radio at the time of the 2016 Referendum would not have been surprised at the vote for Brexit, nor the Tory gains in the so called 'red wall' at the 2019 General Election. Nationally if the BBC is out of touch with the political temperature of the nation then by embracing its local newsrooms it need not be.

Making the right cuts.

Gillian Reynolds was right to argue that the BBC has always treated its local stations 'as if they were Dickensian orphans, unwanted, without status or value' (Reynolds 2020)(v). There are few significant savings to be made. If BBC local radio were scrapped the annual saving of the £127m cost of the service would reduce the licence fee by five pence a year and the BBC would save under four per cent annually; this is no golden egg (BBC Annual Report 2019/20) (vi).

The current proposed ten percent cuts will do damage, but local editors tell me it is do-able if done right. The BBC should limit savings in its newsrooms and programme teams. The financially efficient unified programme schedule introduced across all stations at the start of the coronavirus Pandemic should be made permanent. It offers a route to develop for more local programming at morning peaks in presently underserved communities, even if this is at the expense of limited afternoon programme sharing elsewhere *(Daily Telegraph, May 2020). (vii)*

By accident or design, BBC local radio has recreated the classic sound of ILR from the 1980s, often with the same presenters, and although there are no new public RAJAR figures because of the Pandemic I believe it will prove popular.

As the BBC centrally embarks on new savings targets it should re-examine local radio working practices which have much to offer the networks and is perhaps one of the reasons it has been kept at arms-length from

Broadcasting House. For example, the upcoming major changes to its network radio journalism staff (The Guardian, September 2020)(viii) could be informed by analysing local radio in which staff regularly produce audio, video, online and social media content

Diversity; Not Just a Black and White Issue.

One charge that cannot be made about BBC local radio is that it represents a metropolitan liberal elite. Local Editors are largely state educated with many from working class backgrounds and 14 per cent from BAME communities (Media Info)(ix): two of them joining BBC local radio as recruits to local Asian programming in the 1980s. Stations were quick to creatively tackle diversity when limited independence was offered by Tony Hall in 2018 to allow them 'do more to reflect the diversity of our communities' (Hall, 2017)(x). The subsequent axing of the all-England evening sequence replaced by local programmes saw one third of the shows presented by new BAME presenters (McCarthy, 2020)(xi).

Diversity includes age, gender, geography, disability and social background and BBC local radio has a track record of innovative programming and recruitment, playing an important part in social cohesion in places such as Leicester. In the past where funding has been supplied for one-off diversity schemes the jobs ran out when funding was ended but individual local editors often self-funded retention by creative use of local budgets. The BBC's new diversity funding should be applied across BBC local radio as a way of encouraging a wider social intake into the corporation. While the BBC is to be applauded that half of its staff are based outside London it should be noted that nearly all the decision makers are still in London; local radio bases offer an opportunity to build a widespread but virtually connected management.

Deeper audience connections.

Listeners to BBC local radio are more likely to older and working class than audiences to the BBC networks, indeed BBC local radio extends the reach of BBC radio with over 2. 2 million of its 6. 7 million audience never listening to other BBC stations (BBC). (xii)Through its 36 English stations the BBC has an opportunity to reach out into communities, breaking out from its London or Manchester centric mindset. For Network Radio there is ample opportunity to present and produce programmes in these multi-media centres across the country. If Nick Robinson can present the *Today* programme from his basement, as he did during lockdown, why can't any network programme be based in or be broadcast from any city with a BBC studio base in any of the four nations?

Technology could be harnessed to bring the BBC closer to its audiences, regional TV newsrooms could be split across local radio newsrooms with the opportunity to develop on-demand audio, video and social media service. The BBC shied away from online local TV news in 2008 when the newspaper industry successfully lobbied government that it was about to massively invest in local TV (Guardian 2008)(xiii). It failed to do so, and the BBC should re-visit this idea to connect with the smartphone generation.

The BBC should also embrace community radio offering a branded BBC local news service to stations, regular commissioning of content and assistance with mentoring and training.

Listen local, think national and global

As it reaches its centenary in 2022 the BBC still has an important part to play in a post pandemic UK. However, when decisions are made on cuts and new investments the BBC should safeguard local journalism and look to local radio and its studios as a potential vehicle to build deeper audience connections for its networks. The footprint of local radio should be expanded to underserved towns while the BBC should spread itself more evenly across the country using its local stations as production hubs. After a half century of being on the fringes of the BBC, local radio ought to be brought in from the cold to form a central plank in the rebuilding of the corporation.

About the Contributor

Dr. Liam McCarthy worked for the BBC between 1978 and 2008. He was Editor of three BBC local stations, Leicester, Nottingham and Sheffield and Head of BBC Local Radio Training. In 2020 he completed a PhD at the University of Leicester which examined the social impact of extensive Asian programming on BBC local radio in the 1970s and 1980s

News: Impartiality, Enemies, Balance, 'Troubles' BAME and Wise Men

Introduction

John Mair

Nowhere does the BBC come more into conflict with the political class than in News and Current Affairs. By its nature BBC news is 'fair' so by definition 'unfair' to some; BBC 'balance' means at least one side may end up feeling cheated. Good journalism is mischief (in hiding)and telling truth to power. It does not make for natural bedfellows with those seeking power. Clashes between broadcaster and government are inevitable. The trick is managing them so both survive.

Paul Connew is an old and experienced Fleet Street(as it used to be known)hand. But away from the proprietors, he can see how the national, mainly Right wing, Press is swift to condemn the Corporation and to offer 'unbiased' advice to the New DG. Commercial considerations are, naturally, thinly disguised.

Julian Petley is a long time critic of the ethics of the British media. Now he has a much more clearly defined target. The 'Foxification' of British factual television was once a nightmare, now it is a looming reality. *GBNews* has appeared from out of the woodwork to put some Trumpism into British news. Andrew Neil has offered them great heft by defecting from the BBC. Petley looks into his politics and that of some of the other (mainly ex BBC)individuals coming forth to populate the new Right wing broadcast homes. Their old BBC home was, it seems, certainly not a den of 'lefties'.

Professor Brian Winston takes his own, as ever, iconoclastic look at the history of news in the BBC

During the 'Troubles' in Northern Ireland the BBC-nationally and regionally-came severely under the political and public microscope. A wrong word could mean deaths. Steven Mccabe examines some of the leaning on the Corporation in that time. It emerged-relatively unscathed.

On BAME matters, the BBC has devoted hours ,days, months to anguishing and dreaming up 'diverse ' schemes. Its critics accuse it of 'wokeism'. Barnie Choudhury, a non-white journalist turned Professor, delivers a rather telling allegory of the progress (or not) of two individuals of colour in and out of the Corporation. They are still not getting it or, indeed, getting it right.

Finally a few words of wisdom in an afterword by Britain's most distinguished political historian Sir Anthony Seldon on the value he has got from the Corporation in his lifetime in education. He bookends this fissiparous collection very well.

Chapter 16

Waking up to a Beeb bashing breakfast

As a media commentator, broadcaster and former Fleet Street editor, Paul Connew has been a far from uncritical defender of the BBC. Here he samples how the Tory press greeted the new Director General

The August 30th edition of *The Mail on Sunday* was clearly intended as a warning shot across Tim Davie's bows with added hope of rendering his breakfast indigestible.

Timed two days before he took over as BBC Director General, Davie would hardly have been expecting a warm welcome from the *Mail* , but the scale of the assault probably did surprise Auntie's commercially savvy incoming chief. It was almost an old *Mirror*-style 'Shock Issue' saturation job.

'TOP TORY LAUNCHES TV RIVAL TO WOKE WET BBC', roared the splash, focusing on the hope of Sir Robbie Gibb, the Beeb's political head honcho before becoming Theresa May's communications director, of launching a Right leaning 24-hour channel.

The sub-heading on the MoS front page read: 'Murdoch also plans news channel in wake of Rule Britannia debacle'.

Moving inside Davie was treated to 'From the Left and the Right two political heavyweights on why the BBC's lost the plot', above a column by former Labour Home Secretary David Blunkett under the headline 'Angst-ridden and middle-class, they ignore the values of those who pay their salaries'.

Back to the Last Change Saloon

The right hand side of a double-page spread filled by David Mellor (in pre-Antonia de Sancha scandal days the 'Last Chance Saloon' Tory Heritage Secretary and now the *MoS* classical music critic). The headline declaration: 'As a Minister, I defended the BBC against Thatcher, now I'd abolish the licence fee'.

For good (or bad) measure the paper's polemicist-in-chief Peter Hitchens opened his column with: 'Why are arguments about the love of country always held between BBC-type Britain-hating pinkoes, embarrassed by their own nation, and shouty jingoes, who never think about what patriotism really means'...

If that wasn't enough Beeb-bashing for one issue, the *Mail on Sunday* leader was headlined: '*Reckoning at last for arrogant BBC*' opened with 'The BBC is at last facing its comeuppance after years of unpunished arrogance, behind what it thought was the impregnable wall of the licence fee. For decades it has been the playground of Left-wing bohemians forcing their narrow view of the world on listeners and viewers'.

It closed with: 'Maybe there is just time to recover some of its lost status, but it will need to be very quick and very humble if it is to do so'.

The hottest seat on Planet Media

Well, without suggesting Tim Davie was spooked by the *MoS*, the new DG proved himself quick and relatively humble in his first response to taking one of the hottest (but still most prestigious) chairs on Planet Media.

So much so the *MoS's* sister title *The Daily Mail* even mused in a leader: 'Could it be that the BBC finally has a Director General prepared to listen to his core audience? On his first day in the job, the noises coming out of Broadcasting House about Tim Davie were certainly encouraging.'

Such ephemeral flattery won't fool Davie, a man with a pedigree of global deal-maker at the BBC and untrammelled by the editorial heritage of most of his DG forebears.

He will have noted, too, the September 5th edition of the aforementioned *Daily Mail* featured a fascinating self-interview by that former BBC doyen John Humphrys under the banner headlined 'My Wake Up Call to the Woke BBC'. (See the Introduction to this book)

Land of Hope and Fury

But even among many BBC journalist friends of mine there is an acceptance that, in the age of *Netflix, Amazon, Apple, You Tube* et al, the Davie skill set might be the right one for the BBC's battles ahead. (Indeed, some senior BBC journos I know have privately admitted to me their regret Davie didn't get the top job after an impressive stand-in role in the wake of the Savile scandal fallout that eventually saw Tony Hall appointed DG.

Davie displayed his nimble touch with a smart compromise that largely defused the *BBC Proms Rule Britannia* and *Land of Hope and Glory furore* and deserved to satisfy all but the most tone deaf Brexiteers. A chuckle here for the Twitter wag who dubbed Boris Johnson's interventions 'Land of Hopeless Tory'.

By the same token, Davie's acceptance that the BBC's comedy output is probably too Left wing and could do with some Right wing diversity would have struck a popular chord with the public. (OK, OK, I know, where is there a rich vein of right wing comics and scriptwriters to mine?).

Having taken a sizeable pay cut from his £642,000 salary as *BBC Studios* boss to become DG, Davie was also savvy to outlaw BBC editorial stars coining in hefty personal commercial deals with outside corporations that could be the subject of critical BBC news content.

Smart, too, to crackdown on BBC news staff pumping out personal political views on social media while, rightly, defending the outspoken Twitter activities of Gary Lineker, who isn't on the BBC staff and whose sports presenter credentials aren't compromised by his political opinions.

A winter warning

By mid-September the BBC Annual Report and the list of the corporation's highest earners was guaranteed to spark negative headlines and trigger phone-in show fury and add to the pressure on its new DG. But he handled it more adroitly than Lord Hall.

Without doubt Tim Davie is facing, as per the title of this book, a winter of discontent. Budget cuts and job culls will continue. But will it necessarily be as severe a winter as media weather forecasters predicted?

OK, the Over 75s licence issue won't go away. Neither will the highly-contentious issue of 'decriminalising' non-payment of it.

But, despite the occasional outburst from some Tory backbenchers, the Prime Minister and his cabinet have gone relatively quiet, at least for now.

Word reaches me that, for once, the Prime Minister has put the arm on his arch BBC-hating chief adviser Dominic Cummings to ease up on the anti-BBC 'briefings' to favoured media outlets. Less of the The Dom's 'whacking the BBC' exclusives to the *The Sunday Times* Tim Shipman for the moment, apparently.

Still trusted in time of crisis

Could it be that a beleaguered Prime Minister whose poll ratings and public trust levels have collapsed has come to his journalistic senses and realised that he's facing a far bigger winter of discontent crisis than Tom Davie at the Beeb? Not least when BBC news viewing figures, even among the elusive younger age groups, have been temporarily boosted during the Covid crisis, confirming it remains the broadcaster of choice for millions in a time of dire national crisis.

Certainly some senior Tories, among them former 'Deputy Prime Damian Green, a former BBC employees, continue to press the point that, even as a Trumpian/Cummingsian diversion tactic, stepping up attacks on the BBC may no longer be the way to go for a government slumping in the polls, a Prime Minister losing public trust faster than 'Auntie's' overall ratings, backbench revolts over international law breaching and the looming economic avalanche of a No Deal Brexit winter.

The reason, perhaps, why a couple of Tory editors have latterly taken down the anti-BBC tone level a notch.

Down the line it might help Davie that, back in the 1990s, he was a local Conservative council candidate and, although he's remained strictly shtum at the BBC about his political leanings, the internal speculation places him as a liberal Tory at heart. Which further undermines the popular argument that the corporation's upper echelons are dominated by left wingers, despite the record of senior BBC political execs switching to key No 10 roles with Tory PMs.(see Chapter 2 in this volume)

It may also help that Tim Davie is a scholarship boy, the first to go to university (Selwyn College Cambridge) in his family, in his future dealings with No 10. In 2022, when the BBC celebrates its centenary, he will also have to start negotiations over the future of the licence fee from 2027. He's already indicated he favours its survival, although even some of his greatest admirers wouldn't gamble their shirts on him winning that one.

The deal maker's crunch test

But it's just possible that in a post-Brexit Britain (and if Boris Johnson remains Prime Minister, a longshot in itself) Tim Davie, the global deal maker, can flog the idea that a nation in search of a major new role on the world stage should ambitiously support its most revered international institution and champion a commercial/cultural combination BBC that isn't totally eclipsed by Silicon Valley's tech titans.

In a thoughtful September 1st 2020 piece on the BBC website, the Corporation's media editor Amol Rajan (ex editor of *The Independent*) set out the challenges Tim Davie can't personally control. That the BBC is no longer in a dominant position in entertainment or sports broadcasting and that the 'most powerful companies in human history are competing with the BBC for eyeballs and attention'.

Rajan also focused on the key challenge that could come with the BBC appointment that is strictly in the gift of the Prime Minister - the next chairman to succeed Sir David Clementi in February.

At the time of writing, hot favourite is Boris Johnson's former boss at the Daily Telegraph Charles Moore (now Lord Moore of Etchingham). Shurely shome mishtake in *Private Eye* parlance?

To appoint Margaret Thatcher's biographer, the epitome of a hunting, fishing, shooting Tory toff, and a man once prosecuted in the magistrates court for a protest non-payment of the BBC licence fee would do more than provoke beyond-satire guffaws. It would seriously undermine BBC staff morale.

No Moore cronyism

Witness Moore's recent writings suggesting the government should 'help to decolonise the BBC in a dignified manner…more like British imperial decline than the fall of the Soviet Union'. Or his depiction of it as 'culturally woke, pro-Remain, credulously green and anti-market'.

For his part Boris Johnson would be wise to beware how it would play alongside the cronyism stench increasingly dogging his government in the court of public opinion, particularly over dubious Covid crisis contracts and appointments (step forward, Baroness Dido (Dud?) Harding.

Let's bemoan the absence of robust media heavyweights like Lionel Barber and Andrew Neil among the favoured runners.

The headline on Amol Rajan's analysis ran: '*Tim Davie's hellish new job as BBC director general*',

But not half as hellish as Boris Johnson's and who'd bet against Davie lasting longer as DG than Boris as PM?

About the Contributor

Paul Connew is a media commentator and advisor, broadcaster, former national newspaper editor and Mirror Group former US bureau chief. A regular columnist for *The New European* and *The Drum* and a commentator on media and political issues for the *BBC, Sky News, CNN, Talk Radio, Times Radio, al-Jazeera* and *Australian Broadcasting.* Connew has been a contributing author for six previous books in this series.

References

1-Tim Davie speech to BBC staff, 3 September 2020. Available online at https://www. bbc. co. uk/mediacentre/speeches/2020/tim-davie-intro-speech date accessed 3 September 2020.

2 Bauer closes dozens of regional radio stations in England and Wales, The Guardian, 31 August 2020. Available online at https://www. theguardian. com/media/2020/aug/31/merger-of-bauer-local-radio-stations-criticised-as-cultural-vandalism date accessed 5 September 2020.

3 Who Owns the UK Media, Media Reform. Available online at https://www. mediareform. org. uk/wp-content/uploads/2019/03/execsumFINALonline2. pdf dated accessed 4 September 2020.

4 UK newspaper publisher Reach to cut 550 jobs, Financial Times, 7 July 2020. Available online at https://www. ft. com/content/e36ab119-cccf-4159-8cbd-54f29e022520 date accessed 1 September 2020.

5 Reynolds, Gillian (2020) Is the BBC still in Peril? Yes. But it always should be, Mair, John with Bradshaw Tom, Is the BBC still in Peril? Notes for the new Director General Tim Davie, Goring: Bite-Size, pp. 30-34.

6 BBC Annual Report 2019/20, p. 44 & p. 153. Available online at https://www. bbc. co. uk/mediacentre/latestnews/2020/bbc-annual-report-2019-20 date accessed 15 September 2020.

7 BBC to focus more on Brexit-voting towns in overhaul of local News, Daily Telegraph, 20 May 2020. Available on line at https://www. telegraph. co. uk/news/2020/05/20/bbc-focus-brexit-voting-towns-overhaul-local-news/ date accessed 1 September 2020. 8 Radio reporters to be axed by the BBC and told to reapply for new roles, The Guardian, 13 September 2020. Available online at https://www. theguardian. com/media/2020/sep/13/radio-reporters-to-be-axed-by-bbc-and-told-to-reapply-for-new-roles date accessed 14 September 2020.

9 Analysis of BBC local radio contact detail via Media. info, for example BBC Radio Leeds. Available online at https://media. info/radio/stations/bbc-radio-leeds date accessed 4 September 2020.

10 Tony Hall on the future of BBC local radio, BBC Press Office, 8 November 2017. Available online at https://www. bbc. co. uk/mediacentre/speeches/2017/tony-hall-local-radio date accessed 14 September 2020.

11 Connecting with new Asian audiences: BBC local radio 1967-1990, Liam McCarthy, University of Leicester PhD. Available online at https://leicester. figshare.

com/articles/thesis/Connecting_with_New_Asian_Communities_BBC_local_radio_1967-1990/11798622/2 date accessed 14 September 2020.

12 BBC Local Radio, Information to suppliers for Radio, June 2019, https://www. bbc. co. uk/programmes/articles/1bKMM37GhWK1v1hbKMPt1Vv/bbc-local-radio (Accessed 28 August 2020).

13 BBC Trust rejects corporation's £68m online video plans, The Guardian 21 November 2008. Available online at https://www. theguardian. com/media/2008/nov/21/bbc-trust-local-online-video-plans date accessed 15 September 2020.

Chapter 17

Foxification: Just What a Divided Country Doesn't Need

Hot on the heels of the non-story about the *Last Night of the Proms* comes the announcement of two new 'news' channels which will 'balance' the allegedly over-liberal BBC. However, the accusation of BBC bias is highly questionable, and the new channels threaten to replicate the rampant ideological bias of most of the UK national press says Professor Julian Petley.

All too neatly coinciding with the confected press outrage over the *Last Night of the Proms* came the news that two Fox-style 'news' channels were being planned for the UK. One of these is being considered within Rupert Murdoch's *News UK*, which in May hired David Rhodes, a former *Fox News* executive and president of *CBS News*, to devise the project. This apparently has the backing of Lachlan Murdoch, although currently it is unclear whether what is being planned is a traditional TV news channel or an online-only operation. *News UK* is already developing broadcasting experience with *Times Radio* and *TalkRADIO*, and as the latter has recently increased its video offering, its presenters could possibly become TV pundits. (Incidentally, this is not the first time that Murdoch has shown a desire to introduce such a channel, as back in 2003 he began manoeuvring to 'Foxify' *Sky News,* although this move was successfully thwarted [Petley 2003a, 2003b]).

The other proposed Channel is *GB News*, which acquired a broadcast licence from Ofcom in January 2020, and emanates from the company All Perspectives. This is jointly owned by Andrew Cole and Mark Schneider, respectively current and former directors of *Liberty Global,* which owns *Virgin Media* The company's largest shareholder is the US billionaire John Malone. The largest individual landowner in the States (with 2.2m acres) and widely known as the 'cable cowboy' (Littleton 2016) he is a member of the board of directors of the Cato Institute and donated $250,000 to Donald Trump's inauguration in 2017. He chairs *Liberty Global* and also the parent company of the *Discovery* television network, which is in discussion with *Liberty Global* about a possible tie-up with *GB News*. Andrew Cole, who sits on the board of *Liberty Global,* informed his

LinkedIn followers that the BBC was "possibly the most biased propaganda machine in the world" and asked them to watch out for "the launch of a completely new TV news channel for the UK – one that will be distinctly different from the out-of-touch incumbents". He added: "The people need and want this new perspective" (quoted in Waterson 2020a). GB News has also hired former *Sky News* executive John McAndrew and appointed Angelon Frangopoulos, the former head of *Sky News Australia*, as chief executive.

'Opinion dressed as news'

With utter predictability, the announcements about the new channels were greeted with hoots of glee by the BBC's many enemies in the national press. For example, *The Daily Mail*, on 29th August, announced that "the race is on to bring a US-style news service to Britain" and quoted an 'insider' to the effect that it "will be less Left-wing and less woke than the BBC ... Just by taking a centrist line it will seem more to the Right because the others are so much to the Left". The following day's *Mail on Sunday* quoted a 'source close to *GB News'* as stating that "the channel will be a truly impartial source of news, unlike the woke, wet BBC. It will deliver the facts, not opinion dressed as news". It also published an editorial headed *"Reckoning at Last for Arrogant BBC"*, which crowed that the Corporation "faces not one but two new rivals to its increasingly inadequate and openly biased news and current affairs operation, with its ranting out-of-control presenters and its slanted views of the world".

Of course, whether one regards the BBC in these terms depends entirely on where one stands, and it is thus hardly surprising that papers which stridently support not simply the Conservatives but the Right wing of that party should view it as Left-wing. (Exactly the same ideological conjuring trick is played in the US by *Fox News,* whose claim to be 'fair and balanced' depends on the canard that it is providing the 'balance' to the 'left-wing' news provided by *NBC, ABC* and *CBS).* Furthermore, these papers have a vested interest in destabilising, and indeed delegitimising, a competitor, whilst their complaints about 'ranting' and 'opinion dressed as news' are simply par for the course in terms of the kind of hypocrisy and double standards that one has come to expect from what the former Conservative Prime Minister Stanley Baldwin identified as "not newspapers in the ordinary sense [but] ... engines of propaganda" (quoted in Black 2019: 121). However, because these anti-BBC stories are taken by the government, entirely cynically, to represent 'public opinion' (never mind that many of them actually originated with its own operatives in the first place) and are then used to justify anti-BBC legislation, they have to be engaged with, however dishonest and self-serving they are.

Almost all reliable and academically rigorous research (which completely rules out of court the reports produced by *Newswatch* and anything emanating from the 'Tufton Street mafia', all of which is, of course, meat and drink to the anti-BBC press) strongly suggests that the BBC is not biased to the Left, and that where bias does exist, it is actually to the Right, broadly speaking, although not necessarily deliberately so. The literature on this subject is far too large to adumbrate here, going back as it does to the Glasgow University Media Group *Bad News* studies which began in 1976, but the series of edited collections of which this one is a part contains a number of enlightening contributions to the subject such as Lewis (2014, 2015), Petley (2014) and Gaber (2015).

Enter Sir Robbie

Particularly interesting in this context is the fact that the *Mail on Sunday* article quoted above noted that one Sir Robbie Gibb was "spearheading a drive to raise funds for *GB News*" and that Andrew Neil "tops Sir Robbie's wish list for the news channel".

Gibb is currently Senior Adviser at the public relations firm, Kekst CNC, before which he was Director of Communications at 10 Downing Street under Theresa May. However, prior to that he had had a very considerable BBC career as a political journalist. During his time at the Corporation he was variously deputy editor of *Newsnight* and edited the *Daily* **and** *Sunday Politics*, *The Andrew Marr Show* and *This Week*. By the time he left he was head of the BBC's Westminster political programmes team.

This is actually a less uncommon institutional trajectory than might be supposed, given the incessant clamour about the BBC being a hotbed of leftists. For example, in February 2011 David Cameron appointed a then-editor of *BBC News*, Craig Oliver, as Andy Coulson's replacement as his Director of Communications. In May 2008, BBC political correspondent Guto Harri became Director of Communications for Boris Johnson when he was Mayor of London, and when in 2012 he was appointed Director of Corporate and Public Affairs for *News International*, he was replaced by Will Walden, a BBC news editor at Westminster. Later Walden ran Johnson's transition team at the Foreign Office and was his principal political and media advisor during the EU Referendum campaign. Of course, one cannot necessarily read off people's political beliefs from their career trajectories, and there is no suggestion that any of these individuals was anything other than impartial during their BBC careers.

A committed Conservative

However, Gibb himself has never made any secret of the fact that he is a committed Conservative and ardent Brexiteer, although according to former BBC colleagues, when he worked for the Corporation his commitment to impartiality was not in question. However, from an article which he wrote in *The Sunday Telegraph* on 30th August 2020, it is abundantly clear that he thought the BBC itself was far from impartial. Thus he claimed that it had been "culturally captured by the woke-dominated group think of some of its own staff. There is a default Left-leaning attitude from a metropolitan workforce mostly drawn from a similar social and economic background".

However it would have been difficult for Gibb to conceal his own political background. During the 1980s he was vice-chair of the then notorious Federation of Conservative Students (disbanded in 1986 by Tory party chairman Norman Tebbit for being too extreme). In the late 1990s he worked as a political advisor and head of staff to the then shadow chancellor, Francis Maude, **and in** 2001 he played a key role in Michael Portillo's unsuccessful leadership bid for the party.

A profile in *The Evening Standard* on 25th March 2019, also noted that he is a close friend of Andrew Neil, at whose house in the South of France he sometimes holidays with his family, and whose 'politics and political analysis he held in high regard' whilst at the BBC.

Not a man of the Left

However, Neil is another figure that makes the claim that the BBC is institutionally biased to the Left difficult to sustain. In his career at the BBC, albeit not as a member of permanent staff, he played an absolutely key role in its coverage of politics, at one time or another presenting *Daily* and *Sunday Politics*, *This Week*, *Despatch Box*, *Politics Live*, *Straight Talk with Andrew Neil* and *The Andrew Neil Interviews*. But although he is a formidable interviewer who has interrogated those on the Right as fiercely as those on the Left, and although, characteristically aggressively, he objects on Twitter to having particular political views ascribed to him, it is safe to say that he is not a man of the Left. He was editor of *The Sunday Times* from 1983 to 1994 (during which time it consistently ran stories hostile to the public service broadcasters), and in 1996 he became chief executive of the Barclay brothers' Press Holdings group of publications, which has included at one time or another *The Scotsman, The Sunday Business/The Business, The European* and *The Spectator* (of which he became chief executive in 2004). He became chairman of Press Holdings in 2008. The majority of these publications are Tory-supporting (or were, in the case of those that have ceased to exist), and Neil himself has made no secret of his views on topics as varied as climate change (Neil 2013), HIV/AIDS (Neil 1996; Neil 1997: 430-41), Scottish independence (Withers 2020, O'Callaghan 2020) and Carole Cadwalladr's investigations into the role played by data harvesting and dark money in UK politics today (Mayhew 2018).

That one simply cannot imagine people with views as far to the Left as Gibb's and Neil's are to the Right occupying such key positions in the BBC should (but undoubtedly will not) serve as a considerable corrective to claims that the BBC is institutionally biased to the Left. However, senior BBC journalists have told me that the Corporation has been perfectly happy to have Gibb and Neil on board as it has helped to deflect precisely such criticisms. Indeed, after Owen Jones complained in *The Guardian* on 1st April 2018, that Neil routinely uses his Twitter account to 'promote right wing causes', former BBC editorial director Roger Mosey wrote in the *New Statesman*, 3 May 2018, that 'the BBC secretly enjoys assaults like that, which undermine the usual claim that it is controlled by liberal lefties'. Similarly, Peter Wilby (2019) quoted a source who had worked on Neil's programmes as stating that the BBC "treats him as a protected species. With a Tory government in office, it worries about attacks from the right and what they mean for its future funding. Neil is their defence against allegations of left-wing bias."

This presumably goes some way to explaining why, according to *The Daily Telegraph*, 9th September, the new director-general, Tim Davie, offered Neil a 'higher profile job' than the one he had before *The Andrew Neil* show was taken off air in March 2020 because of the pandemic and permanently cancelled in July as a result of budget cuts. As the paper noted: "Mr Davie's attempt to lure Neil back is a demonstration of his determination to shut down criticism of the corporation over a perception of a Left-wing bias. Neil has been described as the 'antidote to the woke brigade' and is considered sympathetic to Brexit" (Southworth and Mendick 2020). Entirely characteristically, the paper omitted to mention its own very considerable role in creating this 'perception' in the first place. However, the BBC has now lost Neil for good, as on 25th September it was announced that in the new year he would be launching what the *Guardian*, 25th September, called "a new right-leaning opinionated rolling news channel … as a rival to the public broadcaster and Sky" (Waterson 2020b)

Towards the extreme centre

The problem is, however, that in pandering to those who accuse the BBC of being 'left-wing', the BBC has shifted the fulcrum of political debate on its channels inexorably rightwards, or towards what Tariq Ali (2018: 2) has called the 'extreme centre'. It may also be the case that the BBC sincerely believes that it is reflecting a new right-wing consensus. This, I would strongly suggest, is exactly what Neil has in mind when he states in Waterson (2020b) that the new channel "will champion robust, balanced debate and a range of perspectives on the issues that affect everyone in the UK, not just those living in the London area" – in other words, the dread 'metropolitan liberal elite' bogeyman.

However, the fact that the opinions expressed by the majority of national newspapers are overwhelmingly right-wing and that the Tories have a majority of 80 seats in the Commons does not constitute evidence of such a consensus – it is simply the consequence of how most of the national press is owned and run, and of the first-past-the-post voting system. On the contrary, the country has never been more divided – whether in attitudes to devolution, Brexit, the pandemic, the legal system, and indeed the BBC itself, among many other things. As such, it desperately needs the Corporation to adhere to a notion of impartiality which does not involve simply balancing moderate right-wing views against more extreme right-wing ones and throwing in the occasional liberal or left-wing view for ballast And the very last thing it needs are opinionated news channels replicating the Fleet Street echo chamber and creating yet more silos in which people only ever encounter views which they already hold.

References

Ali, Tariq (2018) The Extreme Centre: A Second Warning, London: Verso.

Black, Jeremy (2019) The English Press: A History, London: Bloomsbury Academic.

Edwardes, Charlotte (2019), 'The inside track on Robbie Gibb … the man putting words in Theresa May's mouth', The Evening Standard, 25th March. Available online at https://www.standard.co.uk/news/politics/the-inside-track-on-the-man-putting-words-in-theresa-mays-mouth-a4100251.html

Gaber, Ivor (2015), Beeb bashing by the right: is it justified?, in Is the BBC in Crisis?, Mair, John, Tait, Richard and Keeble, Richard Lance, Abramis: Bury St Edmunds pp 190-4.

Gaber, Ivor (2017), BBC is not biased, but its idea of the 'centre' is now tilting to the right when the UK is tilting to the left, The Conversation, 24th July.

Gibb, Robbie (2020) The BBC has a real chance to reform after losing sight of its purpose, *The Sunday Telegraph*, 30th August. Available at https://www.telegraph.co.uk/news/2020/08/30/bbc-has-real-chance-reform-losing-sight-purpose/#:~:text=Jump%20to%20navigation-,The%20BBC%20has%20a%20real%20chance%20to,losing%20sight%20of%20its%20purpose&text=What%20the%20Rule%2C%20Britannia%20debacle,they%20are%20supposed%20to%20serve. (£)

Jones, Owen (2018) If the BBC is politically neutral, how does it explain Andrew Neil?, *The Guardian*, 11th April. Available at https://www.theguardian.com/commentisfree/2018/apr/11/bbc-andrew-neil-media-politics

Lewis, Justin (2014) How the BBC leans to the right, in Is the BBC in Crisis?, Mair, John, Tait, Richard and Keeble, Richard Lance, Abrams: Bury St Edmunds pp 114-20.

Lewis, Justin (2015) BBC bias revisited: do the partisan press push broadcasters to the right?, in The BBC Today: Future Uncertain, Mair, John, Tait, Richard and Keeble, Richard Lance, Abrams: Bury St Edmunds pp. 182-9.

Littleton, Cynthia (2016) John Malone: 'cable cowboy' faces the test in rounding up the right mix of assets', *Variety*, 15th March. Available at https://variety.com/2016/tv/features/john-malone-liberty-media-charter-communications-1201729414/

Mayhew, Freddy (2018) BBC's Andrew Neil deletes early-morning tweets calling Observer's Carole Cadwalladr 'mad cat woman', *Press Gazette*, 13th November.

Mosey, Roger (2018) Why Owen's attack on Andrew Neil secretly delighted the BBC, *New Statesman*, 3rd May. Available at https://www.newstatesman.com/politics/uk/2018/05/why-owen-jones-s-attack-andrew-neil-secretly-delighted-bbc

Neil, Andrew (1996) The great AIDS myth is finally laid to rest, *The Sunday Times*, 23rd June.

Neil, Andrew (1997) Full Disclosure, London: Pan Books.

Neil, Andrew (2013) Andrew Neil on Ed Davey climate change interview critics, BBC News, 22nd July. Available at https://www.bbc.co.uk/news/uk-politics-23405202

O'Callaghan, Laura (2020) Andrew Neil sends clueless SNP supporters into frenzy – 'What will your currency be?', *The Daily Express*, 25th August. Available at https://www.express.co.uk/news/politics/1326856/andrew-neil-twitter-scottish-independence-supporters-indyref-currency

Petley, Julian (2003a) Foxy business, Index on Censorship, Vol. 32, No. 2 pp 17-22

Petley, Julian (2003b) The wrong medicine, British Journalism Review, Vol. 14, No. 1 pp 81-5.

Petley, Julian (2014) Facts, informed opinion and mere opinion, in Is the BBC in Crisis?, Mair, John, Tait, Richard and Keeble, Richard Lance, Abrams: Bury St Edmunds pp 121-33.

Southworth, Phoebe and Mendick, Robert (2020) Andrew Neil turns down BBC to head up new television channel, *The Daily Telegraph*, 25th September. Available at https://www.telegraph.co.uk/news/2020/09/25/gb-news-andrew-neil-turns-bbc-head-new-television-channel/ (£)

Waterson, Jim (2020a) Rivals plan Fox News-style opinionated TV station in UK, *The Guardian*, 29th August. Available online at https://www.theguardian.com/media/2020/aug/29/rivals-plan-fox-news-style-opinionated-tv-station-in-uk

Waterson, Jim (2020b) Andrew Neil launches 24-hour news channel to rival BBC and Sky, *The Guardian*, 25th September. Available at https://www.theguardian.com/media/2020/sep/25/andrew-neil-launches-24-hour-new-channel-to-rival-bbc-and-sky

Wilby, Peter (2019) More than a spectator: the rise of Andrew Neil, *New Statesman*, 17th April. Available at https://www.newstatesman.com/politics/media/2019/04/more-spectator-rise-andrew-neil

Withers, Paul (2020) Andrew Neil sends Scot independence fans into meltdown – confronts them with simple facts, *The Daily Express*, 21st September. Available at https://www.express.co.uk/news/politics/1338218/andrew-neil-news-scottish-independence-snp-nicola-sturgeon-mike-russell-scotland-deficit

Chapter 18

BBC: It's (Still) the News, Stupid

What is the BBC for? To educate, entertain and inform --- but state funded journalism, however organised, is fraught says the Lincoln Professor Brian Winston, a former television producer himself. We need to rethink the BBC's fundamental rationale.

The apparent hostility of this "administration" towards the BBC is too inchoate, puerile, maleficent and reckless to be worthy of rebuttal. But the Corporation, a creature born of electromagnetic spectrum scarcity nearly a century ago, has always been vulnerable to improper government meddling. Now, as its foundational rationale has been comprehensively destroyed by a changing technological reality, in this age of media (over?-) abundance, even if the authorities were enlightened and supportive, positive rethinking would still be urgently required.

In the Beginning . . the Physics,

On 1st January 1927, the BBC came into existence as the result of an arrangement which kicked an essential problem raised by the need to exploit wireless telegraphy for the mass of the King's "subjects" (as the Royal Charter which did this has it) into the long grass.[33]

Here was a military technology which depended on a natural resource – a type of electromagnetic radiation – which was limited by physics. Its reduced accessibility was thus in contrast to the virtually unlimited availability of the means required by all other media of expression from paper, pens and paintbrushes, through printing presses, theatres and stadia to photography and film.

Despite (or because of) their abundance, governments have always sought to control, by one measure or another, the content produced by, and communicated through, all these means. The wireless and the television which followed these older media were quite another matter. The naturel resource on which broadcasting relied – unseen and generally pretty

---

[33] https://www.bbc.com/historyofthebbc/research/royal-charter

inexplicable except to physicists – needed careful allocation if it was to function effectively.

And Who Was to Do the Allocating?

Governments are usually rather insatiable when it comes to opportunities to govern. And with radio waves, in addition to the inescapable need for bandwidth organisation was the added factor that the technology, developed for naval ship-to-ship and shore communications, was anyway, effectively, already _their_'s: a military asset.[34]

For authoritarian regimes, radio spectrum allocation was no problem and, as they lacked any commitment to free expression in whatever form, nor was the control of content. Broadcasting was a gift, a ready platform for government propaganda.[35]

The allocative function was self-evidently also required in the representative democracies but, given their commitment to human rights, the content control of broadcasting was obviously less legitimated. Balancing a right of free expression against the basic injunction that the exercise of that right does no harm had always been a problem.

It had taken centuries of effort to achieve any semblance of solution to the conundrum this poses and agreements on the issue remained -- and remain -- unstable. (In fact, currently, we can see the consequences in the newest [social-] media of abandoning the requirement of balance. That will have to be fixed but that is another story.)

At the time of radio's arrival – and still in significant part to the present for the older media -- freedom of content has been limited by the laws of defamation, sedition, obscenity and blasphemy. (Only blasphemy has been formally removed.)

Censorship by other means?

Anyway, the allocative function did not necessarily require any further content control of broadcasting. Censorship was, de facto, a separate business, but it was nowhere so regarded and with the allocation of bandwidth came the regulation of awardees' output. Censorship beyond the constraints of the law, to one degree or another, proved irresistible. This

---

[34] Beck, A.H.W (1967). WORDS AND WAVES. London: Weidenfeld & Nicolson, pp.96 _et seq._
[35] Goebbels, Joseph (1938 [1933]) 'Der Rundfunk als achte Großmacht', _Signale der neuen Zeit. 25 ausgewählte Reden von Dr. Joseph Goebbels._ Munich: Zentralverlag der NSDAP.

could be covert, as in the United States where broadcasting licences were awarded in the 'public interest, convenience, or necessity'.[36] This meant, beyond the law -- and regulations to maintain technical standards -- conviction of any criminal offence, for example, would cost you your licence. By a brilliant sleight of hand, the vetting of content, which might be potentially deemed to offend the ill-defined 'public interest' test was left to the licensees. The system was therefore censored – heavily so – by internal 'compliance officers', leaving the US government could happily parading the fig leaf of compliance to its own constitutional requirement that it 'make no law abridging the freedom of speech'.

Britain freer? The BBC experience.

In the UK, at its most permissive -- that is, for the press – free expression had come to mean that it be subject to 'no prior constraint', i.e.: censorship. But other media could be licensed in various ways and their content chilled by the threat of the removal of such permissions. At its most extreme, live theatre was overtly subject to, exactly, prior constraint - - the censorship of all scripts intended for public performance by the Lord Chamberlain's office. As this name indicates, censorship was a time-honoured function of the royal government. But it also reflects the state's critical interest in (and patronage of) culture – especially the so-called Court Arts (for example the ballet).

In 1926, then, the modern British government had allocative reason and censorship precedent when it came to organising broadcasting. But the institution it created in 1927 – the BBC – , tended, as far as content was concerned, more to reflect theatrical practice rather than press 'freedom'.

The Corporation's archives reveal, however tacitly, the brilliance with which such control of the output has been exercised. The absurdist public scandals of interference by the PostMaster General, the minister responsible, in the late 1920s were soon replaced by covert meddling which seldom occasioned notice. Crassness has been, and is still, the exception; but the consequence would seem to be that deep within the BBC's DNA is a certain wariness around adopting the press's hard fought-for role as public guardian.[37]

---

[36] *Communications Act of 1934*, ch. 652, 48 Stat.1064 (codified in 47 U.S.C. §§ 151-611 (1994); *Radio Act of 1927*, ch. 169, 44 Stat. 1162 (repealed 1934).

[37] See, eg: Bell, Tom, (2016). The BBC: Myth of a Public Service. London: Verso,

Only news..

But, note, these incidents, known and hidden, are primarily related to news and current affairs provision. Of course, there have been controversies but they have been of a curtain-twitching kind (currently in the guise of anti-"woke" brouhahas); but, until the current spate, they posed no existential threat. Indeed, before the BBC acquired a measure of the common touch in the 1960s, its taste was sufficiently patrician and its behaviour so snobbish, that complains could be brushed off – or brushed under -- the carpet of its elaborate complains procedures.

But the supposed 'protocols' that protected it from detailed interference are withering, Its freedom, because of its funding, is not as other media freedoms and it is uniquely susceptible to political pressures. By law, after all, the current iteration of its Charter and Agreement,[38] gives the Minister of Culture – the Post-Master General's successor in office -- endlessly detailed oversight of the BBC's work; and politicians are thus entitled to question its performance too.

It's the news stupid...

However, the news etc more than taste etc is the Corporation's Achilles heel. Just as the allocative and censorship functions need to be separated, so too does this de facto division of the output. In short, the BBC's existential problem is the news (etc) not its output overall. State funding inevitably contaminates news provision in a democracy but the provision of circuses et al, as part of its general duty of care for its citizens, can be a legitimate function of any state and always has been. European performance culture in particular has been enriched by the Court Arts and by Courtly patronage. And to this day, out of general taxation, such state support continues.

Of course, the distribution of such funds, via the Arts Councils, say, occasions disputes and disagreements – rightly so. And here funding is, as with all other direct beneficiaries of state largesse, always subject to threat. But their institutional existence is not fundamentally jeopardised as a consequence of the public content they enable. Only the BBC is thus exposed and, essentially, only then only because of the news.

---

[38] https://www.gov.uk/government/publications/bbc-charter-and-framework-agreement

News & state don't mix?

The provision of news in a democracy, crucially, cannot be a state function. To fund it out of general taxation is possible but, as with the state support of the local press in some Scandinavian countries, this must be done 'blind', e.g. : what's the circulation of the paper? is the test for qualification, whatever its politics etc. Otherwise, it is unacceptable.

So, for example, rethinking the licence fee to make it a tax sensitive to income levels a la Sweden will not remove the threat because using any hypothecated tax – e.g. the BBC's licence fee – is far too much in plain sight. It must create threats to independence, specifically to news provision. By contrast, tax money, if awarded blind to content, can make good lacuna in a country's cultural provision generally.

The BBC has since the 1960s set its face against the 'super-serving' of the elite which would result from its shedding the news and becoming a species of an elitist 'arts council of the air'. But that worry ignores the democratisation of taste which has occurred over the last half-century. Radical scholars[39] have long since won the battle to expose the class-based prejudices underlying any Leavisite division of 'low' and 'high' culture.[40] Now, our rock-and-roll heroes get knighthoods as readily as Royal Academician artists. Lacuna can be a matter of challenging the market-place of the popular – which the contemporary BBC has shown itself to be rather adept at doing – as much as it is in providing Court Arts coverage. 'Culture' now is marked with the smallest, most demotic of possible "C"s. And therein perhaps lies the Corporation's best defence against the forces of darkness.

Tony Hall Culture Vulture?

At the outset of Lord Hall's tenure as Director-General there was some talk of the BBC being the platform enabling the outreach programmes of all state supported cultural ventures to maximise audiences. Were 'culture' suitable broadly defined as being, firmly, all that is not by bread alone, and – crucially -- were the hypothecated tax to be replaced by content-blind state funding -- a truly 'world-beating' second century could thereby be ensured for the Corporation. As it is, the current threats are pretty

[39] e.g: Hall, Stuart and Whannel, Paddy (1964). *The Popular Arts*. London: Hutchinson; Hoggart, Richard (1958). *The Uses of Literacy*. Harmondsworth Middlesex: Penguin; Williams, Raymond (1961). *The Long Revolution*. London: Chatto & Windus.
[40] e.g: Thompson, Denys (ed.) (1964) Discrimination and Popular Culture Harmondsworth Middlesex: Penguin

irresistible. But the BBC's enemies only have real purchase only because: its the news, stupid! Let that go, the centrality of the Corporation's role in our national life could be secured and enhanced.

About the Contributor

Brian Winston holds the Lincoln Chair at the University of Lincoln. His latest book, *The Roots of Fake News* (with Matthew Winston) is published by Routledge.

Chapter 19

Balance, bias, and the precious perils of 'impartiality'

New Director General Tim Davie says his top priority is to renew the BBC's commitment to impartiality. 'Bravo' says Juliet Rix, but this may not be as straight-forward as it sounds.

It is hard to over-estimate the importance of a universal source of unbiased news and analysis – to the maintenance of standards in public life, to democracy, to our very health and safety.

For nearly a century the BBC has been the closest to this ideal of any major media organisation in the world – and the world has known it, envied it, and relied upon it when their own countries had no such service.

Even today the BBC is far and away the most trusted news outlet in the UK – and indeed in the USA too.

In recent years, however, 'Auntie's' reputation as the steady relative who can always be relied upon has taken quite a beating, for reasons both real and cynically political.

Though it has had many trials and tribulations in the past - and it is inherent in its role that it comes into conflict with governments of the day – the BBC is undoubtedly at greater risk today than ever before. To survive it must be its very best self – a paragon patently worth preserving.

To tweet or not to tweet?

The new Director General Tim Davie says that his first priority is to renew the Beeb's commitment to impartiality. Three cheers – well, probably. He will start, he adds, by clipping BBC journalists' social media wings. Three cheers again – well, maybe.

How will social media rules be applied?

Would it be reasonable, for instance, for the BBC to impose restrictions on freelancers paid a pittance for occasional contributions? As one of them, I would say the answer is clearly no. Key BBC personnel like political correspondents, on the other hand, could and should be required to observe rigorous objectivity and keep their opinions to themselves.

But what constitutes an opinion? Some things are obvious – party political partiality, unevidenced criticism or approval – but would it be an opinion to say that the 2020 exam results process was a shambles? Although government ministers may disagree and we can argue about causation, I would say that this is not an opinion, but is – in fact – a verifiable truth.

And this brings us to what we mean by impartiality.

Caution and carelessness

I worked full-time for BBC Current Affairs as a young journalist in the second half of the Eighties. Towards the end of the decade I watched with concern as the BBC became simultaneously both over-cautious and a little careless.

The over-caution arrived with DG John Birt, whose approach to current affairs was didactic. I remember a senior reporter on *Panorama* returning to his desk after a meeting with the bosses. He had proposed a particular investigation (I don't recall what). "They asked me for the script," he said, "I thought they were joking and I laughed, but they weren't joking. I said I could hardly have a script before I'd done the investigation. They replied, straight-faced, 'no script, no budget'". He sat down defeated and over the succeeding year, the programme was slowly neutered.

The other change is, I believe, one of the (many) roots of the current impartiality problems. When I started at the BBC, there was a clear divide between journalists and pundits. Journalists reported; pundits were asked their opinion.

"And what do you think?"

As an obsession with 'going live' grew, reporters were more and more required to improvise, answering questions live down the line. Increasingly correspondents were even interviewed by programme anchors in the studio – just like pundits. In this setting, they were – and are – frequently asked, "And what do you think…?"

Correspondents are indeed experts in their fields, often more broadly well-informed than many pundits, but this question should set red lights flashing. If a journalist is routinely asked their opinion in the course of their job, you can hardly blame them for giving it.

So what is impartiality – or perhaps we'd better start with what is it not? It is not avoiding offending people, it is not ensuring no complaints, and is not giving equal airtime to each side of an argument. Impartiality may include, as Tim Davie has said, reflecting the concerns of all of your audience, but not uncritically, not by percentage of airtime, not through the answers given, but through the questions asked.

Balance and bias

The key to impartiality – or objectivity - surely lies in rigorous, wide-ranging, informed and thoroughly researched reporting - without fear or favour – of the truth or, with honest caveats and the available evidence, as close to the truth as can be established.

The BBC has now admitted to having got it wrong on climate change by constantly pitting pro climate change scientists against climate deniers without pointing out the growing mountain of evidence piling up on one side. A news report that repeats a statement (no matter who from) that is known to be questionable or untrue, should immediately state its questionability or evidence its untruth.

It has been considered inappropriate to say Donald Trump and Boris Johnson lie. Why? They do. This is an amply verifiable, easily evidenced, fact. Their elevated positions are surely not reason for blind respect, rather reason to inform the millions over whom they have power of the character and behaviour of their leaders.

Truth delayed is truth denied

Impartial journalism speaks truth to power, and about it. It investigates thoroughly (and without a pre-written script). It interviews critically, calling out inaccuracy with evidence. And it reports with caveats, not relying on some separate 'reality check' or independent fact finder (admirable and necessary those these are) to do the job at a different time with a different audience.

I'm not saying this is simple – or cheap. And therein lies another of the roots of this problem. An under pressure programme can easily set up a couple of pundits with opposing views. Properly researching the issues so both can be held to account on the facts takes resources – something of which the BBC has been shorter and shorter in recent years.

But resourcing impartiality should be the top priority. Presenters and reporters need the time and back-up to be comprehensively informed and impeccably briefed. And they must be able to challenge power with confidence.

Impartial imperative

Davie will need not only to be transparent, scrupulously fair and almost impossibly clear about what constitutes a transgression; he will also need to be ready to robustly defend the BBC and individual journalists when they come – as they will – under political attack.

There are thugs at the door who would like to see 'Auntie' both bloody and bowed – or more subtly deconstructed and disappeared. To resist she will have to be strong, confident, and sure of her ground.

The BBC's survival as a universal source of unbiased news and analysis is imperative.

I wish Tim Davie wisdom, resilience – and a barrel-load of luck.

About the Contributor

Juliet Rix is an award-winning freelance journalist working for national media including the Guardian, Telegraph, Times, and Radio 4, writing on topics from health and social issues to travel, arts and culture. She began her career at the BBC, in television then as a radio foreign correspondent.

Chapter 20

Shot by both sides – the challenges faced by the BBC during 'the Troubles'

Nowhere did the BBC's reputation for impartiality come more under strain than in the Northern Irish 'Troubles'/Civil War. The BBC in Northern Ireland held the line between competing communities, armed paramilitary groups and successive Westminster government ministers who criticised it. Dr Steven McCabe....

'*Shot by Both Sides*' the 1978 single by post-punk Manchester-based group Magazine, written by Howard Devoto and Pete Shelley, is based on an argument concerning politics the former had with a girlfriend who claimed, "Oh, you'll end up shot by both sides." Sang by Devoto with rasping contempt, so *de rigueur* of the period, '*Shot by Both Sides*' includes the lines, "I wormed my way into the heart of the crowd, I was shocked to find what was allowed, I didn't lose myself in the crowd" This neatly encapsulates the quandary faced by the BBC in reporting on events around the 'Troubles' in Northern Ireland .

'The Troubles' for beginners

The United Kingdom (UK) had not experienced large-scale civil disturbance for over two centuries. According to McKittrick et al, (2007) 3,720 people died as a result of the conflict, and as many as 50,000 people were seriously injured (Cain website). The origins of disturbances in Northern Ireland lie in the civil Rights marches which drew inspiration from the United States (McCabe, 2019). Treated with suspicion by many within the Unionist community, leaders were accused of using long-standing grievances experienced by Catholics on jobs and housing to agitate for reunification of Ireland. Attacks by 'loyalists', as well as police officers (Royal Ulster Constabulary, [RUC]) increased tension.

Such tensions were the catalyst to 'ethno-nationalist' hostility between communities that'd simmered since Northern Ireland's creation in 1922. Ten deaths and hundreds due to attacks by loyalists on Nationalist communities in Derry and Belfast in August 1969 created a sense of the Stormont government, led by James Chichester-Clark, unable to maintain law and order. A request was made to Labour Home Secretary, James Callaghan, to deploy troops to assist who decided that control of security become the responsibility of the Army General Officer Commanding Northern Ireland.

'Operation Banner' commenced, the longest ever continuous military deployment in British history. Press interest in Northern Ireland intensified. The BBC, providing regional coverage in 'The Province', was 'on the ground'. However, as the Corporation discovered, reporting from 'within' posed significant quandaries in achieving the objective of presenting news from all perspectives.

The truth, the whole truth and nothing but the truth?

It's safe to assume everyone involved in reporting on the 'Troubles' believed their overriding objective was understanding of issues by viewers. However, simply presenting 'facts' was far from straightforward. As veteran BBC news reporter Noel Thompson explains, the frenetic pace of events frequently resulted in news stories being altered up to the point of broadcast. Thompson acknowledges that an environment created challenge in assembling the salient facts and ensuring absolute objectivity.

Commentators who've worked in Northern Ireland attest to difficulties in gaining access to representatives from organisations engaged in defence of their communities. Others believed them to be 'terrorists'. Irish nationalists largely, though not exclusively, Catholic, considered partition 'unfinished business'. Smaller Irish Republican paramilitary groups, such as the INLA (Irish National Liberation Army) existed but PIRA (Provisional Irish Republican Army) was the most dominant and active.

Unionists, primarily Protestants, believed Northern Ireland should remain part of the UK. Loyalism manifested itself in a variety of paramilitary organisations. These included the UVF (Ulster Volunteer Force), UPV (Ulster Protestant Volunteers, UDA (Ulster Defence Association), LVF (Loyalist Volunteer Force), Red Hand Commandos and the Ulster Resistance.

Early months demonstrated a ferocity borne of embedded historical enmities following partition. However, incidents involving the British army led to the darkest and most deadly years of 'the Troubles'. Shootings by 1st Battalion, Parachute Regiment, of unarmed civilians in Ballymurphy in Belfast in August 1971 and the Bogside in Derry in January 1972 combined with haphazard use of internment, hugely increased bombings and shootings by PIRA. Inevitably, Loyalists responded in equal measure.

Making sense of unfolding events is a challenge to any news organisation. Dealing even-handedly with conflicting views of perceived injustice problematic. Presenting the story impartially essential. BBC reporters though sympathetic to the victims of violence, recognised that atrocities were not motivated by criminality, evil or psychopathy. Regardless of how repugnant some viewers found the implacable opinions of those either engaged in, or at least supportive of, carrying out acts of terrorism, the BBC's reportage should, at the least, acknowledge grievances.

Not fully exploring the motivation to engage in violence by the BBC would undermine its integrity as an honest news organisation. Being judgemental or over-simplifying unfaithful to journalistic endeavour. Moreover, disregarding protagonists engaged in violence risked incurring their wrath. Crucially, whatever revulsion engendered, paramilitary groups in Northern Ireland were supported by communities they 'served'.

Contradictions and conundrums

Those interviewed for this piece stressed that not posing difficult questions to those supporting violence intended to inflict suffering on the 'other side', was to risk being seen an apologist. Every statement and question had the potential to be loaded and all reports, no matter how rapidly produced, the potential to make matters worse not better. The rapidity with which events occurred meant that the intended message was not universally well received by all sections of the viewership.

Tribulations were experienced by all broadcasters in Northern Ireland. However, for the BBC the issues were complicated by its role as a public service broadcaster and the fact its funding came from licence payers. The BBC in Northern Ireland was frequently the target of opprobrium from governments; both Labour and Conservative. Though it is widely applauded as upholding exemplary standards of journalistic integrity, the BBC soon discovered that its most vociferous critics, and capable of making life very uncomfortable, were not those wielding guns and explosives, but UK ministers

Robert J Savage's *The BBC's Irish Troubles: Television, Conflict and Northern Ireland* (2017), is a *tour de force* in analysing the role of the BBC in, what was a pre-digital age, television reporting of the conflict. Savage, a Professor of Boston College, adopts a careful and deeply considered perspective of the way in which the BBC, a 'national treasure', comparable to the National Health Service according to some, achieved the objectives of reporting on conflict in Northern Ireland whilst attempting to displease as few viewers as possible.

The 'Oxygen of Publicity'

That Margaret Thatcher, on becoming Prime Minister in May 1979, had deep antipathy towards the BBC, a news organisation she viewed saw as too liberal and too accommodating in allowing Irish, republican, terrorists the 'oxygen of publicity', was no surprise. Losing closest advisor and friend, shadow Secretary of State for Northern Ireland, Airey Neave, to an INLA car bomb driving out of the Palace of Westminster in March 1979 increased her distrust.

Whatever thoughts Mrs Thatcher possessed as to the ability of the BBC to report on events in Northern Ireland were further undermined following an incident in the County Tyrone village of Carrickmore in October 1979. A *Panorama* film crew (including Jeremy Paxman) making a programme in the Republic of Ireland, were tipped off to the presence of hooded IRA gunmen carrying out checks on traffic in Carrickmore. Contrary to existing rules, the BBC crew filmed them. Though the film was never shown, Mrs Thatcher, according to well-placed sources, went "scatty".

Following Carrickmore, the Chairman of the Governors of the BBC, Sir Michael Swann, was informed, in no uncertain terms, by Home Secretary William Whitelaw of the government's anger. The BBC would need to demonstrate in future it was not giving publicity to the IRA. The remainder of Mrs Thatcher's period as PM was characterised by continuing spats with the BBC. She intrinsically distrusted the BBC as being too left-wing and, as far as reporting on events concerned with the conflict in Northern Ireland, unwillingness to portray terrorism by Irish Republicans as simply acts of criminality. As the hunger strikes in 1981 ironically demonstrated, attempts to portray those engaged in such act as criminals, and continuing the policy introduced under the previous Labour government, of removing Special Category Status (SCS), introduced in July 1972 by Conservative William Whitelaw, to all prisoners serving sentences in Northern Ireland for 'Troubles-related offences', profoundly altered the political dynamic.

Ed Moloney, in his excellent chapter, '*Closing Down the Airwaves: the story of the Broadcasting Ban',* described the policy introduced by Douglas Hurd in October 1988 of the voices of PIRA or its political representatives, Sinn Féin not being allowed to be broadcast on television or radio. Though not a direct consequence, this policy followed the bombing of a bus carrying British soldiers near Ballygawley, County Tyrone, on 20th August when eight were killed and 28 injured. Moloney believes this ban to be, "the most stringent controls imposed on the electronic media since the Second World War."

In the light of the eventual Good Friday Agreement on 10th April 1998 achieved under Tony Blair's New Labour government, it's easily forgotten that it was not only Conservatives who felt loathing for the BBC. Labour, in power between 1974 and 1979, found the BBC's role in reporting on Northern Ireland problematic. One politician in particular, Secretary of State for Northern Ireland between September 1976 and May 1979, Roy Mason, who believed a solution to the conflict would be achieved through tougher security, the use of covert forces, and criminalisation, is especially notorious for his public contempt for the BBC.

In November 1976, Mason attended a dinner at the Culloden Hotel in Belfast to honour the BBC's Director-General, Charles Curran. In his speech at this dinner, Mason made what was described by those attending as a "blistering attack" on the BBC in which he accused it of being willing to act as publicist for PIRA by allowing members to make statements, to include reports of what he believed to be, then, unsubstantiated accusations of misconduct and torture by the security services, (since proven) and of "fomenting divisions with their journalism".

For good measure, and with absolute resonance to the current situation facing the BBC, Mason made clear the threat that if the BBC did not comply with expectations placed on it by the government he belonged to, he'd make it his business to severely reduce its funding for the Northern Ireland region. In effect, telling them to collect and present news in a way favourable to us.

An honourable legacy?

Censorship of news is usually what we associate with dictatorships. When censorship is threatened by a British government, widely acknowledged to be the upholder of integrity, against the BBC, universally regarded as a standard bearer of television journalism, we should experience profound concern. As Savage conclude in his book, the BBC in Northern Ireland during the 'Troubles' "offered compelling coverage of events in very difficult circumstances" and though "confronted with threats, insults, bullying, and finally the imposition of formal censorship [...] did its best to fulfil its mission as a public service."

The BBC in Northern Ireland dispensed its responsibility with courage when required. It reported with utmost attention to veracity and objectivity despite obstacles placed in its path and the pressure exerted by all sides involved. Whatever failures or lapses that may have occurred, its overwhelming adherence to Reithian principles stand out like a beacon in comparison to barbarity of terrorist groups and duplicity of British government ministers.

About the contributor

Dr Steven McCabe is Associate Professor in the Institute of Design and Economic Acceleration (IDEA), Birmingham City University. He has been an academic and researcher since 1987 and has published extensively including, since March 2019, editing *Brexit and Northern Ireland, Bordering on Confusion and English Regions After Brexit: Examining Potential Change through Devolved Power* as well as contributing to *Boris, Brexit and the Media* edited by Mair, Clark, Fowler, Snoddy and Tait, *The Virus and the Media: How British Journalists Covered the Pandemic,* edited by Mair, *The Wolves in the Forest: Tackling Inequality in the 21st Century* edited by Hindley and Hishman and *The Pandemic, Where Did We Go Wrong?* edited by Mair.

References

Cain (2020), *Fact Sheet on the conflict in and about Northern Ireland,* **https://cain.ulster.ac.uk/victims/docs/group/htr/day_of_reflection/htr_0607c.pdf** accessed 28th September 2020

McCabe, S. (2019), 'Northern Ireland, conflict and 'otherness' and the evolution of the Good Friday Agreement', in *Brexit and Northern Ireland, Bordering on Confusion,* edited by Mair, J., McCabe, S., Fowler, N. and Budd, L. Bite-Sized Books, Goring on Thames

McKittrick, D. Kelters, S., Feeney, B., Thornton, C. and McVea, D. (2007), *Lost Lives,* Mainstream Publishing, Edinburgh

Moloney, E. (1991), 'Closing Down the Airwaves: the story of the Broadcasting Ban' in *The Media and Northern Ireland,* edited by Bill Rolston, Macmillan Academic and Professional, Basingstoke

Savage, R.J. (2017), *The BBC's Irish Troubles: Television, Conflict and Northern Ireland,* Manchester University Press

Chapter 21

Star Wars Episode VII: The BAME Force Awakens.

After more than 40 diversity schemes in the past 20 years, the BBC finds itself setting yet more unachievable targets. Professor Barnie Choudhury speaks to two BAME journalists, a generation apart, who say that despite a plethora of initiatives, it remains déjà vu all over again when it comes to real progression at the BBC.

Attack of the clones

In a galaxy far, far away, the BBC, an empire of good people, fights the good fight. It has been trying to up its number of non-white troops for decades. But clever warriors, using Jedi mind tricks, such as freedom of information requests, have discovered that between 2000 and 2014 the Corporation took part in 42 missions, known as diversity schemes. They were meant to increase black and Asian numbers, especially in leadership roles. But the evil Sith apprentices, called gatekeepers, who recruited in their own image, have prevented this from happening. The BBC is at a loss and cannot fathom why mission after mission has failed. So, the generals embark on yet another operation, using the same methods as before, hoping against hope, to crush the Sith rebellion.

The Jedi's story

Malt Wendy* knew he wanted to join the BBC ever since he was five.

"I just knew that I wanted to be a channel controller," said Wendy. "By the time I was 11, I would interview my friends on my father's Grundig tape recorder, a massive thing it was. I edited the tapes, splicing them together, so I could create news and music programmes, which I would record and make my poor mum listen to. At 16, I discovered Radio 4, and I would create schedules of different news and current affairs programmes."

It was 1990 that he joined university radio, graduating four years later, and working in independent local radio before getting a break with the BBC. Once in, Wendy set about learning everything the BBC could offer.

"I would bug the reporters and producers, come in on my days off so I could go to court and learn how to be an ace journalist," he said. "But the sad thing was that no matter how hard I worked, I just couldn't get anywhere."

Wendy recalled that despite having a staff job, showing enthusiasm, dedication and working unsociable hours and long shifts, when it came to being promoted, he was never lucky. Instead, six years later, he had to make a sideways move, on the same grade, to network radio on attachment. After six months, he never returned to his parent station.

"After another 10 years at this network station I was still on the same grade that I entered the BBC," he said. "No matter what I did, I couldn't get promoted. Even though I output edited and acted up, for some reason, I was never good enough to be made substantial."

It was only after his 32nd rejection that he questioned what was happening.

"I sat down one day, and I was so upset, I unburdened myself to a police friend who was fairly senior," Wendy remembered. "My friend started to laugh, and I remember thinking that he was being cruel. He then explained what happened in the Met, which was classed as institutionally racist."

Wendy's friend asked him whether he had a mentor or a champion? When the now 16-year BBC old hand asked what he meant, his cop chum explained it was someone who took more than an interest in another colleague's career. When jobs came up, their network of contacts would know before they were advertised. If someone needed something strategic doing, they would be put in the job-holder's sphere of influence, given opportunities to shine. For Wendy, the penny dropped.

"It was a road to Damascus moment," he said. "I realised that senior white colleagues would bring in their friends, people who went to the same university or children of MPs and celebs, into the newsroom on work experience. Before you knew it, they were getting shifts and then a staff job within months of them arriving. What's worse was that I was asked to show them the ropes, and after a couple of years they leap-frogged me."

Wendy left the network news programme for another, on the same grade. Eight years later, after moving from job to job inside the BBC, the Jedi master remains on the same level he entered it 24 years ago. The structural, systemic, and institutional racism, said Wendy, have defeated him.

The padawan's story

Meanwhile, on another planet in the north of the galaxy is a padawan, a Jedi apprentice who is not, according to the BBC, ready to be a master. Anushka Ivory* joined the BBC in 2013 after completing a journalism degree. She had been spotted by a Jedi master who saw that the force was strong in the young apprentice.

"I was at an awards' ceremony for my university work, but I didn't win," said Ivory. "One of the judges came up to me and said that they thought I should have won, and they were going to use their contacts to see if a big local boss in the BBC would meet me for a coffee and chat."

After a series of meetings Ivory was offered a paid internship. Her role was to bring in stories from her community the radio station could not get. Within weeks, Ivory's stories were leading the bulletins. Her ability to source hard-hitting, human interest and racially diverse stories were followed up by regional television. They ranged from knife-crime to access to gang members. Her reporting was cutting-edge and authentic, receiving plaudit e-mails from her manger and the head of the regional centre. But during one programme debrief, Wendy could not believe her ears.

"One of my colleagues asked how I was getting my stories and whether the people I was interviewing were my brothers, sisters, cousins, mum, dad, aunts and uncles," she recalled. "I was shocked, but then they said, for everyone to hear, 'how do we know that you're not just making it all up?'

Ivory was upset, but she felt unable to say anything because her internship was about to be turned into a contract, and she did not want to spoil her chances. The apprentice believed that if she were white no-one would have accused her of making up her stories.

A few weeks later, a 12-month contract signed Ivory met the Head of Centre for a catchup and explained what had happened. Within days her colleague was made to apologise, which they did half-heartedly, according to Ivory.

After a second contract, this time for six months, the trainee asked whether she could get some television experience. Ivory moved to the regional television newsroom, and once again her access, ability and acumen shone through. Before she knew it, Ivory was producing stories that led the evening news.

"I was able to get stories others couldn't, but I was only allowed to produce. It was as if they didn't trust me enough to be on-screen. Perhaps it was my age because I was only 23. I don't know, I became frustrated and I felt I had outgrown the place."

Ivory spoke to her mentor who advised her not to do anything rash. They said that Ivory was on the cusp of getting a precious staff position in the largest, most revered and best-known news organisation on the planet. But the apprentice ignored that advice and became a freelancer in the national newsroom.

"I knew it was a risk, but I also knew what I had to offer," said Ivory. "I could provide ideas, treatments and access to people they could only dream about."

Many may think this was young arrogance, but Ivory was better than her word, and within 12 months, she won a staff position. A year later, another network news programme snapped her up. Not only that, Ivory became an on-screen talent as well as a producer, bringing in exclusive stories every week.

"I was killing it," remembered Ivory. "You could see everyone was so happy, and my editor kept on telling me how exceptional I was and what a bright future I had in the BBC. I even got shortlisted for a national award."

Yet Ivory found out that she was not being paid as much as her white colleagues who were contributing less than her. By this time other broadcasters approached her to join them, offering Ivory a more senior position and a better wage. She asked for time to think. Two weeks later, they approached her again to ask for a decision.

"I went to my editor and explained what had happened, and I asked them to match the salary and title I was being offered. They asked for a couple of days to see what they could do. They came back and said there was no extra money, but that BBC bosses wanted to do everything they could to keep me and promised me more opportunities. It was all jam-tomorrow. What made things worse was that I know a white colleague was given a pay rise weeks before."

Ivory, the now older padawan, left the BBC after six years and joined the another rebel alliance as a Jedi master.

"You know the saddest part?" asked Ivory. "Once the BBC knew I was leaving, they cut me off. They couldn't wait to see the back of me, after everything I had delivered, it was 'Later, we've got other people who can do what you do'. The sad thing is, if you look at the BBC, they employ young black and Asian people from Oxbridge, middle class, in their own image, who say the right things, but they can't do what I do or get the access I can.

"I grew up on a council estate and know hardship. These guys may be ethnic, but they're hardly a minority. Class matters in the BBC. These guys don't have a clue how to be around people who can't afford a meal and have to do without, so their kids can eat. They don't know what it's like not to have a job and be told they have a mountain of debt. How can they get under the skin of 'their' communities?"

A new hope?

In September 2020, the BBC had a new emperor. In his first speech to troops, Tim Davie, a marketing guru, failed to put diversity as one of his top four priorities. But he said he wanted the BBC to have 20 per cent black, Asian minority ethnic colleagues across the entire organisation. In his first external television interview, Davie told Theresa Wise, CEO of the Royal Television Society[41], "This is mission critical. Some of the editorial decision making, everything that is going on, is utterly dependent on having a truly diverse team. I was very blunt in my first words – don't hire in your own image."

Davie has promised to go division by division to put things right.

"I'm not giving a timing because I want you (divisional leaders) to own it. Accept it's hard, work out what churn do I need in my senior management, how many people out there can I hire? It's granular, it's really detailed work. It's about leadership and accountability. [To] the leaders in the BBC, I have been very direct, you will not be promoted in this organisation without us assessing how happy your staff are, and how you delivered against diversity targets."

Revenge of the Sith?

The problem for the empire is that, as of 31st March 2020[42], the BBC had 329 generals or senior leaders. Of these, just 25 were identified a BAME,

[41]Royal Television Society (2020) *In conversation with Tim Davie, RTS Digital Convention 2020* [online video] Available from https://rts.org.uk/video/conversation-tim-davie-rts-digital-convention-2020 [Accessed 20 September 2020]

[42]BBC. (2020) *BBC Group Annual Report and Accounts 2019/20.* Available at http://downloads.bbc.co.uk/aboutthebbc/reports/annualreport/2019-20.pdf [accessed 20

that is 7.6 per cent of all senior managers. The BBC would not put actual figures on the number of black or Asian senior leaders, or in which divisions they exist, citing that the "data has been replaced with an asterisk where figures are below sample size." A long way from the 20 per cent the emperor expects or will accept.

*Names have been changed to protect the identity of those interviewed.

About the contributor:

Barnie Choudhury is a communications consultant and writes for Eastern Eye, Britain's number one south Asian national newspaper. He was a BBC journalist for 24 years and won several industry awards for his reporting of diverse communities. Barnie is a professor of professional practice at the University of Buckingham.

September 2020]

Afterword

Destroy the BBC, and the Whole World will Lose

Sir Anthony Seldon

This chapter reflects my experience of the BBC from a lifetime spent in education, as a school teacher for 10 years, the head of schools for 20 years, and the Vice Chancellor of a University for the last five years. I write also as a historian of contemporary Britain, and the founder with Peter Hennessy of the Institute of Contemporary British History.

My experience points me to the inevitable conclusion that Britain is now in real danger of undermining a national institution of foundational importance to this country for nearly 100 years of its existence since the BBC was created in 1922.

The BBC has immeasurably enhanced this country, contributing to national cohesion, its international standing, its education, entertainment and tolerance of divergent views. Very obviously, the BBC has not always got it right. But there is a real risk that ignorance will now destroy the greatest treasure in our national life after the Monarchy.

I started teaching at schools in the mid 1980s – Tim Davie, the current Director General of the BBC, was one of my first students at Whitgift in Croydon – and I would regularly encourage my politics and history A-level students to listen to the *Today* programme, *Question Time, Panorama*, and the rich variety of news and politics programmes. It was the height of Thatcher's Britain, and in a polarised country, I judged that the BBC was exposing them to both sides of the argument.

The more I immersed myself in schools, the more I championed the watching of the BBC on television, and the listening to its radio programmes, marvelling at the quality of the production, the genuine excellence of the research, and the diversity of the coverage.

I was able to exploit the new technology of the time – videotapes in the form of VHS and Betamax – to record endless television programmes, which I would drop into lessons as appropriate moments: ditto radio programmes. US politics was one of my core subjects: lessons were greatly enhanced by the students listening to what Alistair Cooke was saying on *Letter from America* the previous week. The television screen and cassette recorder were serious assets for me then, as they still are for teachers, vastly enriched by the output of the BBC.

At my next school, Tonbridge ,one of my jobs was to be in charge of sixth form general studies. That job would've been conceivable without the resource of the BBC, which served up a constant flow of high quality, challenging and inventive programmes which I showed students on the issues of the day, which included unemployment, deindustrialisation, the end of the Cold War, nuclear disarmament and the cohesion of Europe. As a head teacher at Brighton College from 1997, I was constantly encouraging students and staff to watch and listen to the BBC programmes to enrich the life of the mind, which is the core function of education and, later, at Wellington College too.

As head of The University of Buckingham since 2015, I regularly asked international students what attracted them to Britain. The *World Service,* and the quality of the BBC in general, were regular factors they mentioned which formed their sense of Britain as a civilised, tolerant and progressive nation. Strip down the BBC, and the international students who flood into Britain in their hundreds of thousands each year will have a very different, and I believe impoverished, view of the country.

It is as an author and academic about contemporary Britain (I have written or edited over 50 books, ten about recent Prime Ministers) though that I see the BBC playing its biggest part. When I first started taking students to the USA on regular trips from the 1980s, they would comment on the relatively poor quality of US television, and the distraction of ubiquitous advertisements. The greater choice of channels in the US, they felt, was no substitute for what the BBC offered at home. This is the really key point. The BBC provides balance and depth in a dangerously divided world. The damage done by partisan broadcasters in our increasingly polarised world is plain for all to see. The BBC straddles the middle ground. Take it away, and we will become even more tribal.

Throughout history, the decline of nations has been accelerated by those who damage and belittle its culture. This is happening today. Reform the BBC, certainly.

But we should be investing in it, not diminishing it.

About the Contributor.

Sir Anthony Seldon, Vice-Chancellor of The University of Buckingham from 2015-2020, is one of Britain's leading contemporary historians, educationalists, commentators and political authors. He is author or editor of over 50 books on contemporary history, including the inside books on the last five Prime Ministers, Chair of the National Archives Trust, was the co-founder and first director of the Institute for Contemporary British History, is co-founder of Action for Happiness, honorary historical adviser to 10 Downing Street, a member of the Government's First World War Culture Committee, was Chair of the Comment Awards, is a Director of the Royal Shakespeare Company, and was executive producer of the film Journey's End.

Bite-Sized Public Affairs Books are designed to provide insights and stimulating ideas that affect us all in, for example, journalism, social policy, education, government and politics.

They are deliberately short, easy to read, and authoritative books written by people who are either on the front line or who are informed observers. They are designed to stimulate discussion, thought and innovation in all areas of public affairs. They are all firmly based on personal experience and direct involvement and engagement.

The most successful people all share an ability to focus on what really matters, keeping things simple and understandable. When we are faced with a new challenge most of us need quick guidance on what matters most, from people who have been there before and who can show us where to start.

They can be read straight through at one easy sitting and then referred to as necessary – a trusted repository of hard-won experience.

Bite-Sized Books Catalogue

We publish Business Books, Life-Style Books, Public Affairs Books, including our Brexit Books, Fiction – both short form and long form – and Children's Fiction.

To see our full range of books, please go to

https://bite-sizedbooks.com/

Printed in Great Britain
by Amazon

66738328R00086